The Book with Twelve Tales

JOHN GALLAS was born in 1950 in Wellington, New Zealand. He came to England in 1971 and currently works for the Leicestershire Student Support Service. He has published five earlier collections of poetry with Carcanet and edited the anthology of world poetry *The Song Atlas* (2002).

JOHN GALLAS

The Book with Twelve Tales

CARCANET

First published in Great Britain in 2008 by
Carcanet Press Limited
Alliance House
Cross Street
Manchester M2 7AQ

A CIP catalogue record for this book is available from the British Library
ISBN 978 1 85754 875 4

The publisher acknowledges financial assistance from Arts Council England

Typeset by XL Publishing Services, Tiverton
Printed and bound in England by SRP Ltd, Exeter

Contents

Morten Mortenssen the Fat Pig

Morten Mortenssen was a fat pig.
Which was rather the point.
He lived in a paludal paddock
at the back of a cold bungalow
somewhere down the road between
Norre Nebel and Norre Bork,
which was called Sausage Cottage,

where the sun sat in the sky like a frozen backside.

Winter was clangingly long,
like a long piece of frostbitten tin
nailed lengthily over the world,
along which Morten rattled and farted,
sourly surveying the foodless tray of paddock
that was his confines, and his range.
'This,' he grunted, 'is getting on my tits.'

And the icy sky bit the sun tighter and tighter.

Morten blobbed down in his sty,
decorated in a hot, wet cloud of burp.
Straw tickled his testicles. A gleam
of unstrenuous excitement flibbled in his eyes.
His stomach lay like bagpipes in the mud
and hooted complaints and airs of Sir Hunger.
His trotters twitched in a horny not-dance

and a white-meat face watched from the bungalow window.

'Hawgs,' said Niels One, 'can see the wind they reckon.'
He withdrew his pipe and stared at it like it was Philosophy.
'Plugoles,' replied Niels Two. He took his face
out of the kitchen window and sat down at the table
and puffed his pipe. 'If Hawgs cd see the wind' – puff –
'sorsages wd be blue.' He looked long
at the ceiling. 'Mmmmm,' replied Niels One.

Morten fluttered his beautiful white eyelashes.

The next day was clangingly long and cold.
The Nielses stamped across the long, tin paddock
wrapped in matching sweaters and beanies
to stare at Morten's progress. Morten's eyes narrowed.
He heaved himself into a winningly helpless lump,
his trotters in the air for his Cross, his belly awry.
'Aaaaagh,' said Morten. The Nielses looked down,

their pipe-smokes curling past the bum sun.

'Ooooh aaaagh,' said Morten, more loudly.
His tongue hung out in a snotty picture of Starving.
'Mmmmm,' said the Nielses.
Morten waved a futile trotter, cunningly, he thought,
indicating the frozen, unrootleable bloody earth
and dribbled terrifically. 'Yum,' he drooled.
'Hawg,' said Niels One, nodding wisely:

at which Morten exposed his unattractive penis for proof.

'When Hawgs is hungry,' said Niels One,
pointing his pipe-stem at the straining sun,
'the moon'll be a near of corn they reckon
come Lammastide.' 'Ducks,' said Niels Two.
Morten barraged to his feet, impelled by this handy wisdom,
and, in a clicking sort of way, danced out
onto the nailed-tin paddock, where he smacked his trotters

and dropped sad, hot snot onto the icy, bastard world.

By evening, when the stars were stabbing their icepins
through the black fabric of Night, and the deep –
whatever … by then, Morten had his fat head
stuck in a bucket of rotten apples and frozen chips,
baked beans, old cream buns and squashed sprouts,
and was farting happily in the manner of a Melody
while the grass snapped and squidged in frozen horror.

'Ha easy crunch yum chaw chaw,' said Morten cleverly.

The Nielses sat in their condensated kitchen,
a hot water bottle on the table for warmth,
and puffed on their pipes. They communicated
by Smoke-Rings: that a Hawg that cannot rootle
because the world is froze is a peevish Hawg,
a scrawny Hawg and, God Help Us, a mean Hawg.
The little sign that said Sausage Cottage rattled,

and the Nielses saw, smokily, a wolf at the door.

Every day from October to March, under the cold-meat sun,
Morten did his fat, The-Earth-Is-Frozen dance,
threatening, like Salome, to disgruntle Certain People
if he did not get what he wanted. The Nielses,
puffing, steaming, smoking and sermonising,
struggled with a traffic jam of plastic buckets
filled with the neighbourhood's helpful rubbish.

Whereby Niels One developed a hot shiver, and Niels Two a worm.

And Morten Mortenssen burgeoned, flowered and blossomed.
It was nippy and inconvenient to go outside and dance:
but in truth he rather enjoyed hurling his stomach to and fro
and clattering like a submachinegun on the ice.
Unfortunately, May the twenty-seventh was a warm spell.
The paludal paddock softened softeningly
and tasty beech mast and click-beetle grubs
rose to the surface like turds in a puddle,

while the sun rotisseried itself though only at Mark One.

And other nice, green, living things began
to burgeon, flower and blossom. Morten's eyes narrowed.
He had, in fact, Retired from Rootling, realising that
being Fit was inconsequential and dull compared to
being Fat. He stared at the dripping kitchen window
and fluttered his beautiful white eyelashes.
The testicle-tickling straw begot a gigantic, genial fart,

and the sun set like a half-cooked joint, tied up with fog.

Soon it was Very Late in Spring, which was almost
the season when pigs in Morten's Land of Pigs
skipped out to fend for themselves. Morten watched crossly
as the neighbours' fields became dotted with animals
that rootled and snorted for cockchafers and acorns
in the unwillingly reinvigorated grass and brush.
'Bugger that for a game of soldiers,' said Morten,

and he fluttered his eyelashes and waited for his bucket.

But one day the Nielses didn't come.
Morten stuck his snout out into the balmy morning
and dribbled as he inspected the kitchen window.
He tapped his trotter. It went plop-plop in the mud.
He yelped, and lay helplessly in his sty doorway.
He grunted and laid out his extensive stomach.
He staggered along the grass in a fair imitation of faintness

but no one came. The sun lowered itself to watch.

Morten's pleasant pantomime stopped abruptly.
He crapped overflowingly in the potato beds.
He farted at the sun and burped along the hedge.
He stamped, gruntled and snorted with such venom
that the merry-making pigs half a mile away lifted up
their marshmallow ears and looked at each other
with big, glassy eyes. He started towards the house.

'For fuck's sake,' he puffed, 'give me some food!'

Morten mammothed up the front steps, which snapped.
'Lazy bastards,' he snorted. The door was shut.
'Shit,' he burbled, and butted the plywood panels.
And again. Bomp. The door splintered and fell off its hinges.
'Right then,' said Morten, meaning business,
'where's those selfish bloody arseholes.'
Well, they weren't in the kitchen for a start,

though, lit by the enquiring sun, much was.

Flat cans of lager popped listlessly on the table.
Pig magazines limp with condensation on the floor.
Sweaters, socks, beanies and underpants inside out
on the chairs. Charred, greasy pots and pans on the oven.
Shrivelled grilly things under the grill. And
a sink full of fat, Coco-Pops, tobacco-shreds and dishes.
'Oh yum,' said Morten, hauling himself up to snortle.

Then he noticed a meandering stream of vomit on the lino.

'Ahaaa,' said Morten, and trotted after it, lumberingly.
His stomach bubbled and sucked like an emptying bath.
When he got to the kitchen door, the vomit,
which was pink, runny and almost completely blobless,
became rather bloody. A pair of shat-in
shell-suit pants lay halfway down the hall.
Morten stared at them as he wobbled past,

while the sun rolled round the house, curious too.

Sausage Cottage trembled. Morten hauled himself
to the end of the thin, yellow carpet, where he stopped
to worry the blood, which was now glittered with worms,
with his shiny, pumping snout. 'Mmmm,' he said.
His fine sense of smell led him to the bedroom.
He smashed the door down with his cross head.
'Feed me you bastards!' he bellowed. Ah –

the Nielses were lying unslumberlikely on the bed.

Morten narrowed his eyes and tapped his trotter.
The window was blinded with tacked-up binbags.
The sun peeped in round the edges with snoopy brilliance.
The Nielses didn't move. Morten staggered nearer.
The Star Wars sleeping-bags were teeming with worms.
The matching pillowslips looked like blocks of blood.
The Nielses had fallen rather to bits.

'Selfish piles of shit,' said Morten. The sun smiled.

Not feeding a fat, lazy pig is hardly sufficient cause
to be eaten alive. But the Nielses were. Though only just.
Morten, infuriated by the interruption in service,
ate the servants. It took him several days,
but had the advantage of never having to move far.
And then he lay down in a pile of bones and teeth
and licked the blood off the bed-linen, and ate the worms.

Which was where, a month later, the police found him.

They were minded, in their nausea, to arrest Morten
and put him on trial for murder. But that seemed silly
in the broad light of day, of which the sun provided plenty.
Repackaging into Meals seemed like a pretty good alternative.
The Universe, especially the Men part of it,
is indefatigably moral, and Morten Mortenssen
could hardly raise himself anymore to be a stud.

The sun dropped onto the plate of the horizon, well done.

The Mongolian Economy

Long ago – achoo! – in Choybalsan
a pretty woman and a handsome man
got married. Everybody was invited,
and everyone declared themselves delighted.
The bride wore everything. They all had tea.
The yurt extension buzzed with bonhomie,
and then they all went home, and it was spring.

I miss Mongolia. The ouzels sing,
the ermine sniff the sky, the aspens shake,
the goats gambol, the corncrakes corn and crake,
the salmon jump, the camels honk – achoo! –
the marmots scamper round like marmots do,
the snowcock squeals and paddles through the sky,
the sturgeon bubbles up, the cedars sigh,
the honeysuckle swirls, the leopards yawn,
and Nature's children bud and sprout and spawn
till all the world is full of life again:
which also should include the world of Men.

The pretty little yurt stood neat and still
where Hoo (the groom) drove sheep across the hill
and Sim (the bride) made yoghurt in the sun,
which set (the sun): when one by one by one
she lit the candles. Hoo came home. They ate.
The candles sparkled. When the clock said Late
they went to bed. *Let's ride!* said Hoo. He put
a Russian condom on and then his foot
against the stirrup of her thigh and whoa!
they cantered off. They crossed the steppes, then slow
along the Gobi, right up Tavanbogdo,
down the beary forest, through the snow,
splashing up the Tuul and past the plains,
chucking off the bridle and the reins
they galloped into yoghurt hell-for-leather
and jumped the Milky Way – achoo! – together.

And when we can afford to have a child
we'll do it bareback! Sim lay back and smiled.
They blew the candles out and went to sleep.
She dreamed of having twins. He dreamed of sheep.

And summer came like fire. The sick air boiled.
The sheep got Redfly Rot. The yoghurt spoiled.
The pretty little yurt turned brittle-brown.
Hoo rode out across the hill to town
and sold the last spare bags of milk and meat.
He rode back slowly. Withered in the heat,
the yellow plain-grass rattled, scrunched and tore
like paper. Hoo rode on, and wept. He saw
dead marmots in the dust, the little lake
all white and shrunk, the grounded, gasping crake,
the broken thyme, the drooping pines, the sere
and shrivelled poplars, and the trembling deer.

So every day they scrimped and saved: the mutton,
milk and tea; the onions; every button
on their shirts; and every lick of fun.
But when the roiling, red, tendrillious sun
swarmed down behind the plain and darkness dropped
its cool, felt hands across the sky, they stopped
their penny-pinching work, and went to bed.
Hoo took off his hat. *Let's ride!* he said.
They lit the candles. Hoo got out his tin
of Russian condoms, put one on and in
and off they went across the shining earth,
galloping for all they both were worth.

Autumn came and went. The plain went blue
and mushed. The days got shorter. Each day, Hoo
rode off to hunt for marmots in the bogs
and Sim sewed little camels, yaks and dogs
on handkerchieves to sell in Choybalsan.

The winter came like death. The sky began
to sweep and swirl, the plain went stiff and black,
the yurt went white, the felt began to crack,

and Sim sat shaking by the feeble fire,
sustained by lard and pregnant with desire.

One morning as she sewed a marmot skin,
her eye fell on the Russian condom tin,
which stood beside the bed, discretely veiled
beneath a saddle-cloth. The wild wind wailed
around the yurt. The pallid fire-stove guttered.
Sim got up. Her pretty fingers fluttered
at the cloth. She eyed the tin a minute –
opened it – and – there was nothing in it!

Last night ... he had one on ... we rode so far ...
across the plain ... we saw Ulaanbaatar ...
the sky was warm ... we ate the sugared air ...
and sweet, sustaining hope was everywhere ...

The black and hungry truth usurped her brain:
the poverty, the childless years, the pain
of Not Enough. The little camel-train,
embroidered through the lashing, endless plain
with needles made of ice and threads of rain
laughed at her defeat. She looked again –
empty.
        Right. She took the skinning saw
and went outside. Piled up against the door
were forty frozen marmots shot by Hoo.
She ripped one off. She went inside. She knew
she only had a little time: the day
was almost dark and dead. She sawed away.

Hoo came home with nothing, so they ate
a half-thawed marmot. When the clock said Late
they went to bed. *No candles now!* He smiled.
Don't forget we're saving for a child.
He turned away. He frowned. He found the tin.
She held her breath. He slid his fingers in.
The fire flamed up. Now Hoo believed he'd used
the condoms up last night. He was confused.
Of course he was. Imagine his surprise –

9

and huge relief – when there before his eyes
(well, somewhere vaguely in the gloomiment)
was one more johnny! On and in it went.
Yee-ha! he yelled. They started at a trot.
Now Hoo had planned to say that he had shot
his penis off, or had the flu, or mumps,
or spots, bad breath, the Winter Droop, or lumps
around his testicles: so when the load
of fat, white lies was all unpacked, he rode
with extra enterprise and derring-do,
and Sim increased her saddle-squeaking too.
What with the dark, the wild relief, and not
to mention Love itself, they both forgot
that something wasn't right. And as they thumped
along the rushing Khalkhin Gol and jumped
on Soyon's swollen peaks, the marmot's gut,
intolerably strained and wrong, went *phut!*

And thus I was conceived – achoo! – and Van.
Crushed by double poverty – a man
who saves a candle cannot save for twins –
we moved to Sukhbaatar. Dad empties bins.
And mum sews dels. And me? Well, I'm a writer.
I live in London now. It's much politer.
No kids. I went to Sukhbaatar last week
to visit. Their apartment's pretty bleak.
I got this story. Mum and dad looked old.
But pretty happy. And I got this cold.

Rich

'With money you can even buy rabbits' cheese.' Bosnian proverb

How does a drive of grovelling ermine grab you?
And a front door in the shape of two nubile walrusettes
holding the midnight sun aloft and laughing haha?
And a hall heavier than an ice-floe featuring
wallpaper made out of polar bears, crossed fulmar and
a chandelier of a hundred and sixty decapitated caribou?
And a pinous staircase where wolves in tuxedos
serve gin and Oxburgers beneath the music of
a thousand Red-Throated Loons strung
from the ceiling by silver fishing-lines?

If the answer is Pleasantly, then you might
like the house of Zigismund Walrus,
who is arriving even now
in his enlarged Rolls Royce:
but I rather hope it isn't.

He is dressed in a Red Fox coat and a top hat
made out of a harbour of Harbour Seals.
His boots are shiny and made out of something else dead.
He is breathing heavily. His breath is fish and clam.
His stained tusks heave in the air with wet yellowness.
His eyes swim in the smoke from a Chinese cigar.
'Nearly there, my dear,' he breathes at a shivering
Snow Goose he has pulled half onto his knees.
His erection thumps against her neck.
'Don't be frightened.' The sky is dreadfully white.

The ermine scrabble at the door handles and grovel
in a kind of Mexican Wave. Zigismund Walrus
drags the Snow Goose in through the gaping doors.
The walrusettes laugh haha and No.1 Fox says,
'Welcome.' The pinioned Loons shriek.
'Take the lady to the Very White Room,'
says Zigismund Walrus. Foxes scurry her away.
A feather blows on the marble floor.

It would be wrong to say that it was quickly over.
For the Snow Goose an eternity of anything else
would have been shorter. Zigismund Walrus
did not register – through lack of necessity or the
profession of power – Time. But the foxes knew
that it was about twenty minutes,
according to the Musk-Ox-Head clock.

Zigismund Walrus lies on his white eider cushions
and rings the bell for gin and a fresh cigar.
He is satisfied but unflattered by his performance.
The Snow Goose is put in a bag and drowned.
The eider ducks suffocate in silence.
Zigismund Walrus strokes his whiskers and yawns.
His stomach rises like a Zeppelin.
Availability has made pleasure less exciting.
Frequency has dulled his appetites.
Fear has precluded love, obsequiousness friendship
and luxury discernment. He yawns again
and rings the bell for a gigantic iced bath.

And now Zigismund Walrus is bored.

Everything yields to Wealth, says Alberto Blest Gana.
He was speaking of Chile, but the general rule applies.
The rich man's wealth is his strong city, says Proverbs 10:15.
*To be wealthier or more powerful is not necessarily
to be worthier*, says Heloise.

Zigismund Walrus yawns so his tusks tickle the ceiling
and rolls himself out on his Seal Sofa. His stomach
groans a little like an ape lost in the Underground.
'I WANT RABBITS' CHEESE!' he barks.
The foxes mutter, shuffle and enquire:
What why how where.
'NOOOOOW!' Zigismund Walrus stands up,
eclipsing the room with fat. The foxes scatter,
dropping blobs of Oxburger and steely drips of gin
from their trays. Zigismund Walrus smiles.
Evening falls like the House of Usher. Unpleasantly.

Domed into their black puffa jackets, the foxes
hiss across the iron pack-ice on a squadron
of dog sledges. Their wraparound dark glasses
reflect a sliding white line that resembles the purity of Maths.
Their revolvers are too cold to touch.
They are headed towards Arctic Rabbittown
to make cheese. Ten sledges of Lady's Bedstraw
squashed in leather bags slide on behind.
A Lemming Professor of Dairy Studies
from the University of Svalbard,
guarded by foxes with fusils,
hisses along coolly in their midst, crucified to a
handy wooden pallet like a living recipe book.

Arctic Rabbittown is quiet.
Rabbits are lolloping and twitching here and there
amongst the vegetable sheep and tussock.
Some are burping in their holes
or thinking of yesterday in warmish hollows.
The sunlight is mean but not cold.
Rabbit-puppies scramble around in bundles.
Mothers lactate in the buzz of contentment.
Patches of airy snow melt with
the slowness of dying cells.

Everlasting peace is a dream, says Count Helmuth von Moltke.
He goes on to say it is not even a pleasant one,
but the general rule applies.
All we are saying is give peace a chance,
say John Lennon and Yoko Ono.
Peace is in the grave, says Shelley.

Rabbit No. 243 stands up his ears to test
the cold vibrations of morning.
They seem unusual and worrying.
He closes the little lash portcullises of his eyes
and trembles with concentration.
A distant drumming rolls beneath
the chime of his heart. He gasps but does not move.
It is not the clicking groan of shifting ice.

It is not the growl of the sea.
It is not the thrum of evening.
It is not the world turning or
the sun winding its way up the sky.
It is not the grinding of time.
And, being none of these, it is danger.
Rabbit No. 243 propels himself down the hill.
The sky is a grey mist painted yellow.

Zigismud Walrus turns over, steamrollering the softer
wildlife beneath him. Coins fall out of his dressing-gown
and spin on the marble floors. He is sleeping
a dreamless sleep. Whether this be peace,
lack of imagination, contentment, exhaustion
of various kinds, moral bankruptcy, security,
Heaven or Hell, is debatable. I think perhaps now
Zigismund Walrus's money is, without being actually spent,
but, nevertheless, as a most powerful Cause,
Making Things Happen, and the Prime Mover,
who does not have the moralities of Free Will
to arbitrate amongst in the acts and minds of creatures
he has animated for his own purposes,
may take a rest from the world,
having set it on its inevitable course.

The horror! The horror! says Mr Kurtz.

Between 11 a.m. and 4 p.m., when the sun escaped
from the sky like an eye wounded by the world,
eleven hundred female rabbits died, and
sixteen hundred puppies. Three hundred male rabbits,
defending one or the other, went the same way.
No foxes were hurt.
Ten gallons of rabbits' milk was collected.

A huge fire is lit on the ice.
The milk, lying in a vast pan,
begins to smoke a little over the flames.
The foxes, their dark glasses gleaming red,
hurry hither and thither in the milk-fumes

14

like fireflies around a moonlit lake.
The bags of Lady's Bedstraw are pitchforked into the smaze.
Huge spoons stir the milk by a rigging of pulleys.
No.1 Fox chews gum and smiles. The great coagulation,
like the wrong answer to some beautiful question,
is hoisted up and dropped into a bowl of sackcloth.
While it drips and drains, the foxes put on their gloves
and shoot the Professor of Dairy Studies
until he drips like a colander. Then he is thrown,
pallet and all, into a hole in the ice.
Two large bubbles burst in the blood- and milk-thickened air.

Snow begins to float across the ruins
of Arctic Rabbittown. The foxes zip up
their puffa jackets. The cheese drips drippingly.

And nothing shall be impossible to you, says Matthew 17:20.
He is speaking of the Faithful, but the general rule applies.
*The difficult we do immediately: the impossible takes
a little longer*, says Charles Alexandre de Calonne.
*When a distinguished but elderly scientist states
that something is possible, he is almost certainly right.
When he states that something is impossible,
he is very probably wrong*, says Arthur C. Clarke.

Arctic Rabbittown is palled with snow.
The wet white winding-sheet lays
its freezing antiseptic on the torn and
broken flesh already purpled by the wind.
Darkness draws its curtain on the day.
A few rabbits limp across the freezing hillocks
and lie down alone to be asleep
before the sun returns, and after.

Zigismund Walrus wakes like a towerblock.
Parts of him come on; others linger, then, unwillingly,
light themselves to see the so-called labours of the day.
He bathes his tonnage in blue icecubes. Two vixens
wash his tusks and whiskers with seaweed and giggle
as they loofah his thunderously swaying arse.

He breakfasts on a thousand clams,
dribbling onto a silk serviette. Then he dresses,
like the earth putting on weather.

Zigismud Walrus stares at the perfectly cubed
lumps of Rabbits' Cheese. 'Burp!' he says.
The day looks ravishing outside.
He flaps at the cheese. For a moment
there is nothing there. Then he rallies.
'NOW,' he barks, 'FIND ME
1) THE IMPOSSIBILITY OF REVOLUTION
2) THE GREEN SUPPLY OF CREATION
3) THE FISH OF CONTINUOUS APPETITE
4) THE BELL OR IT MIGHT BE A SPRING OF
                                    IMMORTALITY!'

And the walrusettes on his great front door
laugh haha at the golden morning, whose snowfall,
gorgeously lit, resembles a shower of coins,
a kind of Mineral Abundance. Zigismund Walrus
grunts and glares. The foxes leave to find maps.

For God is a consuming fire, says Hebrews 12:29.
He is not speaking about anything else.
God ordered motion, but ordained no rest, says Henry Vaughan.
I was born on a day God was sick, says César Abraham Vallejo.

The Ballad of Lucky Razek

for Clifford Harper

The morning ached with loveliness,
the city burst with light;
the bombs fell with a gentle hiss,
and all the sky was bright.

Lucky Razek stepped outside
and glittered in the heat.
Then, happily preoccupied,
he hurried down the street.

He passed the Mosque of Two Kazims,
its golden domes on fire;
he pattered down the Street of Dreams
beside the razor-wire.

Today he had to buy a hat.
A bomber pricked the sky.
He passed the smoking Laundromat.
A police car hooted by.

So keep your head, the sparrows sang.
A shout. A crack. A spark.
Electric blue. A whoosh. A bang.
He pattered past the park.

Just keep your head. He wiped his face.
A Happy Birthday Hat.
He reached the Victory Marketplace.
He stopped. He smiled. He spat.

He ordered tea and cigarettes.
The sun was made of gold.
Flies flew round like jewelled jets.
I'm twenty-two years old –

and Lucky! Only God knows why.
And God knows everything.
He sucked his tea. A puff. A cry.
The sugar sparkled. Ping!

A tray of glasses hit the air.
He lit a cigarette.
The pieces plinked down everywhere.
Old men played cards. *Not yet.*

The Tigris twinkled in the sun.
He clicked his beads and dreamed.
A pod of dust. A powder gun.
He nodded. Someone screamed.

And while he snoozed a Maori made
a man with paua eyes:
two women in Helsinki played
the start of 'Butterflies':

a boy in Ougadougou took
a photo of his goat:
a girl in Shanghai dropped a book:
an Inuit fixed his boat:

and someone killed a pig in Perth:
a hare stood up and blinked:
a star was buried in the earth:
a fly became extinct.

And then he woke. The Tigris gleamed,
the golden mosque-tops shone;
the old men smiled, the tea-boy beamed.
The sounds of war were gone.

Lucky Razek crossed the street.
The Headwear Paradise!
Elite – Upbeat – Complete – Discreet –
Your Nice-Price Merchandise!!

He whistled round the ziggurats
of beanies, hood and flaps,
sombreros, headscarves, cowboy hats,
and skulls and baseball caps.

New York Jetz. He smiled. He spat.
And *I luv San Francisco*.
Then he saw his favourite hat –
Demolition Disco.

'Try it on,' the hat-man said.
'It's very cheap.' 'Okay.'
Happy Birthday. Keep your head.
A thump. A ricochet.

He propped the mirror up. He twirled.
He grinned. He looked like – *whack!*
A metal breath. The stallcloth swirled.
The mirror-glass went black.

The cap flew off and down he went.
His blood sprayed up the wall.
The money that he never spent
fluttered through the stall.

And all the marketplace was still
and all the world was wrong.
A single burning daffodil.
A patriotic song.

The tea-boy tiptoed through the fire.
The cap was good as new:
hanging on the razor-wire,
electric midnight-blue.

He stopped. 'A man without a head' –
and Lucky's head was gone –
'Do not require a hat,' he said.
He smiled and put it on.

And God saw all the bridges break,
the houses all alight
like candles on a birthday cake,
and all the sky was bright.

The Suspicious Llama

for Michael

There is a small Z road
that loops down a hillside
in Bolivia, and then crosses
a small bridge, and comes to an end
beside a shed and
a bucket of geraniums,
which are the end of Bolivia,
which end is followed by
a small lawn and
a small C road
that is the beginning of Brazil
which slides over a plain
into the arms and space of the people.

The shed is a Passport/Visa and
Customs House for travellers
crossing quietly between Bolivia and Brazil,
and outside, sitting on a chair,
is Alberto Alfredo Acomodadizo,
who is an ant-eater.

The day is warm and very quiet.
Alberto's uniform is carelessly open.
Nothing much passes this way.
Today nothing at all has passed this way.
Alberto waves his tongue at some flies
and scratches his stomach.
He yawns and smiles.
When he is asleep,
his officer's hat falls off.

Brrrrm brrrrm.
Alberto wakes up.
A small cloud of dust rolls down the hillside.
Soon he can hear the tyres crackle

on the gravel near the bridge.
He gets up and buttons his jacket.
He recovers his hat from the geraniums.
An open-topped Lotus pulls up.

The driver is a very fetching llama.
She is wearing dark glasses
and an expensive beret.
Her ears are beautiful.
The Lotus shines in the sun.
Alberto walks a little nearer.

'Where are you going?' he says shyly,
his tongue flickering at the door handle.
'Brazil,' says the llama.
She takes off her glasses and smiles.
'Am I on the right road?'
Alberto blushes at his silly question,
and the kindness of her answer.
'As you see,' he says, pointing his tongue
at the small C road ahead,
sliding over the plain.
They smile together at their
little conspiracy of politeness.
Alberto's watery eyes are bright.
He waddles to the bucket
and moves it out of the way.
The geraniums wobble beautifully.
Alberto waves the Lotus past
and it purrs expensively into Brazil.

The next week the Lotus reappears,
rolling down the hillside in a cloud of dust.
It crackles across the bridge
and pulls up at the shed
where Alberto is watering the geraniums.
He smiles at the beautiful llama.
She is wearing black plastic earrings
and a lemon pashmina.

He puts down the watering can
and walks up to the Lotus,
his tongue curling at the wipers.
'Hello,' he says lamely, and blushes.
'My name is Alberto.'
The llama smiles. Her ears shine.
She smells of Eau de Lima.
There is a crocodile-skin suitcase
on the back seat.
She stretches out a glove to shake his hand.

The next week the Lotus reappears
again. There are two suitcases
on the back seat. The llama smiles.
She is wearing a mohair headscarf
and a necklace that glitters.
Alberto swallows his tongue and says,
'May I look in your suitcases?'
He blushes and waddles towards the car door.
The llama gets out elegantly.
'Of course,' she says.
His tongue curls at the crocodile-skin suitcases.
The llama smokes a Crème de Menthol
while Alberto looks. Nothing.
He moves the bucket out of the way
and waves the Lotus past.

The next week the Lotus is back.
And the week after.
And the week after that.
The llama smokes
while Alfredo searches
an ever-increasing number of suitcases.
Nothing. The llama smiles.
Alfredo waddles away
and moves the bucket
and waves the Lotus past.
The llama waves her glove at him
as she purrs expensively into Brazil.

One week the car comes down the hillside
in a cloud of dust and stops
beside Alfredo's chair.
The llama gets out and lights
a cigarette with a gold lighter.
She looks especially beautiful.
She has a mock-fur coat
and red plastic boots,
a Chanel baseball cap
and diamond earrings.
Alfredo blushes and waddles
towards the car, his tongue
questing at the eleven suitcases
packed on the back seat.
Alfredo searches them all.
The llama wanders about on the small lawn
and smokes with a smile.
Nothing. Some clothes, toiletries,
books, shoes, a camera, a passport,
all in order.
The llama puts up her sunglasses
and kisses Alfredo on the cheek.
'This is my last trip,' she says.
Alfredo blushes and waddles away.
He moves the bucket
and waves the Lotus past.

The small Z road
and the small C road
are empty. The dust settles.
Alfredo sucks his tongue
and sighs. He sits on his chair.
The geraniums wobble beautifully.

Ten years later, Alfredo
waddles into 'The Llama Bar'
in Porto Triunfo.
He has retired. He is tanned.
His pink shirt with lace frontage

is open at the chest.
He is wearing a medallion
of the Angel of Relaxation
and a pair of tight jeans.
His cowboy boots go snap-snap
on the wooden floor.
He orders a bottle of Bonachon Beer.
He sits in the disco light.
He smiles and siphons his tongue
in the beer. An alpaca
in a small leather skirt
crosses her thighs on a bar stool.
Alfredo blushes and looks away.

There, at a private table,
drinking champagne with an armadillo
whose moustache is curled
and whose suit shimmers,
is the beautiful suspicious llama.

Alfredo stands up. He moves
into a darker corner, and watches.
She looks the same.
She laughs and smokes.
The armadillo puts his hand over hers.
She smiles and drains her champagne.
Alfredo watches.
Lines of light loop on her dark glasses.
She laughs softly contralto.
He waddles up to her table.
The armadillo pulls his moustache
and says, 'More champagne!'
Alfredo blushes and takes a deep breath.
'I am not a waiter,' he says.
'I am a Passport/Visa
and Customs House Officer.
Retired. I have the honour
of knowing this lady.
My name is Alfredo.'
He bows slightly.

The armadillo crushes his cigarillo
in a heavy glass ashtray.

The beautiful suspicious llama
smiles at him.
'Ah,' she says. 'I remember.'
Alfredo takes another deep breath.
'What were you smuggling,
all those years ago?'
The disco light revolves its colours.
The armadillo fondles his cufflinks.
The llama leans forward with a tinkle
and whispers champagnely in Alberto's ear.
'Cars.'

The Tale of Tales

1

follow me please we have reached
the River Skut which you can see here
scooting along
rolling its shoulders like a skier
look please at the sun drilling
its yellow hole in the bluegrey sky
and over there a man
with 4 medium fish in a plastic bag
who is walking home with a red beard
just in front of the end
of the row of poplars
flitterfluttering in the breeze
and please especially at his shoes
socks and trousers
which are sopping wet

blackberries explode drupel by drupel

now follow me please a little way
down the riverbank here
and mind the slippery bit
and look over there by that bush thing
I don't know what it is
where you can see another man
with a medium fishing rod
but no fish
in the sunshine on the bank
and please especially at his nice dry
trousers socks and shoes
the poplars creak
and you can see the river scooting along
follow me please

the blackberries shoot purple blobs into the air

2

She pricked her arm
on the prickly palm.
Next
she got a text
from Li Tzu
that said *cnt c u.*
He didn't say why.
Birds of sadness crossed the sky.
She sat in the park
in the dark
wearing her coolie hat
so that
despair
wouldn't nest in her hair.

3

Rakish was an interesting man.
He had no troubles
and he had no god.
So he bought a goat.

4

Suva was fast asleep.
The dark sea lapped at the concrete waterfront.
Rusty ships rolled sleepily in the bay.

Victoria Parade was dead.
The dark sky rolled in bits and pieces
across the sleepy shopfront windows.

The Reverend Sonny Nupenai
in his dark sulu and dogcollar
padded past the ghostly windows of the Wing Ho Café.

Across the still dark glass
his beautiful Chamberlain umbrella
swam like a grouper in nightwater.

He watched himself pad out of one
and into the next sleepy shopfront window
until he reached the beach.

The air was empty and dark.
He stood on the concrete slipway
and put up the harvest of a dead aunt.

It fluttered on its struts in the night.
The rusty ships rolled sleepily in the bay.
He walked along the beach, protected from the moon.

Suva was fast asleep.
Under the dark little canopy of his pride
The Reverend Sonny Nupenai walked towards the sun.

5

Passing through
Oru
on my scooter
I robbed a banjo
off a bench.

When I got
home
dad asked me
if I'd stolen it
and I said No.

6

I got an interview for a job as a baker's assistant in Calcutta.
They said it might not work because my head was made of butter.

7

She sat in the Turkey Café,
wearing a yellow sarong.
Her high smile gave her away.
You can't hide love for long.

She sat on the Senator's yacht
and smiled at the lights of Hong Kong.
She burst in a trumpet of snot.
You can't hide a cold for long.

She sat with the family cat,
while the family played mahjong.
The sprinklers flooded the flat.
You can't hide smoke for long.

She sat in the Turkey Café,
wearing a red sarong.
Somebody sent a bouquet.
You can't hide money for long.

8

for Tamara Romanyk

Apukhtin was having a picnic
amongst the silver birches.
The evening light made stripes
across the mossy grass.
An earwig landed on his arm.
He brushed it away.
It landed on a sausage, dead.
Oh dear, thought Apukhtin
in a wave of tenderness.
Immediately, a swarm of wasps
landed on his crudités.
I shall be kinder this time,
he thought.

9

I call my dog Fried Chicken
Chips and Coke
in case I have to eat him
when I'm broke.

10

ah come dahn outta them mountains
an the snow was flahin an ah wuz kinda cold
an this feller he says
he can rahd mah saddle
fahv tahms in a row
an ah says ahm fifteen
an hes ahl done in baht ten minutes
an ahm near thirty
an he took mah wallet
an ah took his horse
an ah rode on out through the snow
twahds Washingtons Elbow
an ah reckon we come out abaht even
and I reckon well both get on
raht enuf in this world

11

Dr Eckhart is famous
for curing sick men
who do not die.

12

Ali went to the dyer.
He wanted his coat dyed blue.
The dyer sold it to Nasir
and bought a large cockatoo.

Ali went back a week later.
I've come for my coat, he said.
The dyer said, blue is unlucky:
I think we should dye it red.

Ali went back a week later.
The dyer said, Ali, I think
red is a little bit bloody:
I think we should dye it pink.

Ali went back a week later.
Pink is a pain to keep clean.
The dyer shrugged his shoulders.
I think we should dye it green.

Ali went back a week later.
Green is a little passé,
the dyer said. Ali said, and?
I think we should dye it grey.

Ali went back a week later.
Oh grey is a little bit cold.
The cockatoo chuckled and bobbed.
I think we should dye it gold.

Ali went back a week later.
Gold will take far too much time.
The dyer and Ali had coffee.
I think we should dye it lime.

Ali went back a week later.
The dyer had gone to Al-Zed.
The cockatoo looked at him sideways.
Where's my coat, he said.

It is dipped in the vat of oblivion.
The cockatoo bobbled its head.
It has taken the colour of Nothing.
The one I like least, Ali said.

The Monkey's Dilemma

Chuu, a thoughtful, red macaque,
was loping down Shikoku Beach
along the frothy hide-tide-mark

when something caught his eye. He stopped.
He poked his finger carefully
amongst the flotsam. Hm. He hopped

around it once, and scratched his head.
A starfish, wrinkled, flat and pale,
lay on the sand, its limp legs spread

like something two-times crucified,
and half nailed-up again. Sadness
overcame him, and he cried,

O little starfish san – and then,
like something torn, its little mouth
went *tsup*. Chuu frowned. It *tsupped* again.

Chuu hopped round it backwards, sniffed
its gluey air and slapped his nose.
He grabbed a shell and tried to lift

the dry, light, yellowed, o-ing thing
and turn it over. Plop. He jumped.
The turning tide began to bring

its next collection up the sand.
Chuu scratched his ear and frowned. The waves
went *ssss*. He didn't understand –

and thoughtful monkeys like to know
what causes and effects pertain
to things that … well, that *happen*. So

he asked the sea if it would drown
or save his friend the starfish. Answer
came there none. So Chuu sat down

and rolled his eyes. The sky went grey.
He felt the spray fizz round his ears.
He bounced around to ask which way

his friend was heading. *Hoogh*, he said:
starfish san, I'd like to help.
He hunkered closer. *Are you dead?*

The mouth went *tsup*. The sky went black.
Good, he smiled. *Now tell me, shall I*
Leave you here or put you back?

The sea went *whoosh*. Chuu cupped his ear.
But answer came there none. *So shall I*
put you back or leave you here?

No *tsup*. No sign. No nothing. Hm.
Chuu poked it, put his ear against
its flesh and whispered, *Can you swim?*

But nothing happened. Chuu could see
that shortly, when the tide came in,
his own potential charity

would all be swamped by blind events
like sunset, moonrise, winds and tides,
and lose its moral credit, sense

and, therefore, notability,
because its object (starfish san)
could not say thank you, wave, or see

its rescuer, or know he knew,
or register the favour done,
or have a conscientious view,

or actually express one, on
the acts of others (unadvised),
especially after it was gone.

Something, therefore, unexpressed,
might just as well be unconceived.
The monkey frowned and scratched his chest.

Was it selfishness that made
him pause upon the fatal act
of choice? Though Chuu was unafraid

to act, he feared the egoistic
dark, the self-reverberations
of the soul, the altruistic

emptiness, the judgement on
one's deeds deduced from evidence
that, though loosely based upon

the way the world goes, is one's own
ideas. *Oh starfish san,* he said,
and wrung his hands, *if I had known*

that neither God nor anything
that moves or thinks would be with me
tonight upon this beach to bring

some comfort, sign or help to me
I never would have come. He sniffed.
The quiet, blind, advancing sea

washed up his tears. The starfish lay
completely still, or was. The water
ate his feet and hissed away.

What knowledge did he have that might
inform his choice? Well, none. And if
the starfish couldn't set him right

then things looked grim. This little soul
was in his hands, and only luck
could save it. If he gave the whole

conundrum up, he could be blamed
for Death by Doing Nothing. Hm.
Confused, depressed, annoyed, ashamed,

and doubtful of the world and how
it worked, the monkey turned away.
The sky went cold and livid. Now

he had to choose. He slapped his head.
He loped this way and that. He grunted
squealed and cried. And then he fled.

The sky went starry. Chuu came back.
He picked the starfish up and threw it
far into the sea, whose black

and foamy tongues were licking up
the last high-water's flotsam. Answer
came there none: no thanks, no *tsup*,

no lightning, curse, reward or sign
that what he did was right or wrong.
Chuu loped away. A gentle whine

disturbed the moon. Chuu swung his arms
and headed for the twisted trees,
the sweet, familiar fields and farms

of home. The sky went out. The sea
went whispering away. The moon
sailed slowly on. Chuu climbed a tree.

He watched the conscienceless view.
He whispered something thoughtless to
himself. The ricegrass whispered too.

President Kala and Imi the Poet

Wait here, said a woman with an elephant gun.

Imi sat on the rush mat and waited.

Small flies took off and landed sideways
along the smooth white walls.
The sun, shredded through grass slatting,
made lines like bright yellow cotton
along the stamped earth floor.

The afternoon was still and hot.
Birds slept on the lawn. Shadows,
elaborately woven by blinds, slats,
shutters and trees, tipped to one side
and slid, crisscrossing in fretted layers,
along the smooth white ceiling.

Imi waited. She heard each drop
the sprinkler threw amongst the dusty grass.

Follow me. Imi got up and touched her hair.

President Kala's room was yellow.
There were two flags on sticks, a waterbottle,
a cigarette tin in the shape of the Town Hall,
a fly whisk, one glass, a rug on the wall
and a pair of sunglasses on the floor.
                                    Imi waited.
She heard a dog bark far away and a taxi horn.

President Kala came in with a piece of paper.
She picked up the sunglasses and put them on.
She was wrapped in yellow.
It was the national colour.

She looked at Imi through the dark glasses.
Is this yours? she asked. Imi looked at the poem

printed on a sheet of yellowy paper.
Yes, she said. *Then*, said President Kala,
you may have to answer some questions.

A passing car window threw a glittered blink
against the waterbottle and was gone.

In lines 4 5 and 6, said President Kala,
you have written – she cleared her throat
er-huhg er-huhg – I would give for my love
Gao Bilia and Mourouro to my love.

Imi smiled. The rug on the wall
looked like another country from space.

Have you not? said President Kala
her sunglasses inkily dark, her turban gleaming.
Yes, said Imi. *Er-hugh then I must tell you*,
said President Kala leaning forward on her
yellow-cushioned mat, *that I own Gao Bilia
and Mourouro and all the rest of this country
and that therefore you cannot give them
to what you please to call your love.*

President Kala's voice rattled like broom pods.

Imi smiled. It is only a theoretical hyperbole, she said.

It could hardly be anything else, said President Kala,
*as the places you mention
are not yours to give away.*
President Kala shifted her buttocks
on the yellow-cushioned mat.

A fly motored around the top of the waterbottle.

Could it? No, said Imi.
Then why say it? said President Kala.
*It is hardly a measure of love to promise something
that everybody knows it would be impossible*

38

for you to give to someone in whom you are surely
trying to engender trust belief and certainty?

The fly spiralled inside the bottleneck,
its little white suckers pricking the glass.

Is it? asked the President. Her sunglasses beamed black.

It is an expression and measure of love,
said Imi staring at her dusty toes,
especially in poetry, to promise the moon and stars
or indeed the whole world to the object of your love.

Imi took a deep breath. The birds shuffled on the lawn.

It is only a gesture whereby
the greatness of one's feelings
can find expression in writing
by measuring them against
the great things of the world.
President Kala sat back a little.

A shutter creaked so slowly
it sounded like a distant motorbike.

The fact remains, said President Kala,
taking up her flywhisk and thrashing it
at the passing fly which had just
shot out of the bottleneck,
that what you have written is ridiculous, impossible,
impractical and a lie.
                    Imi frowned.
My poem, said Imi, is a world of feelings and ideas
which is not the truth of the world
of possible things, but of
my own heart, seeking to communicate
its love by means of the objects of the possible world
so that it might be at least in part understood.

President Kala smiled and shone bright yellow.

Then you must not include amongst the unrealities
or other-realities of your feelings
my perfectly real cities
and offer them from your heart
when they are actually in my hands.

President Kala sat back on her yellow-cushioned mat.
The sun slid its patterns crisscross along the floor.

Coffee arrived. President Kala took a cigarette
out of the Town Hall tin. The flags hung stickily.
Imi took a deep breath, inhaling
the hot yellow air that helped her.

The cities that I figuratively professed
to give away – *My cities*, said President Kala,
exhaling smoke at the flywhisk and sucking coffee
from her small yellow cup – Your cities,
continued Imi, bowing her head at the yellow turban
shining in the stripy sunlight, are
the objective correlatives to my emotions,
the picture by which my love is figured forth
and thus is capable of being measured, taken,
assessed and, as I have said, understood.

President Kala poured a glass of water
and offered it to Imi.

We have all been to school, said President Kala.
However when the external facts are given,
which are not only the cities that belong to me
but also the spurious act
of your giving them away,
they are not the formula of your
particular emotion, which is, you say, great love.
How can this emotion be evoked by objects
that remind the public only of me and by an act
that is a politically blasphemous fantasy?

President Kala crushed her cigarette butt
in the Town Hall Square, which was
a kind of ashtray area.

They are the symbols or images of my heart,
said Imi, so they are mine to give, really,
as much as my own heart is mine to give.

President Kala finished her coffee.
She put down the cup. Her sunglasses flashed.

The sun sank and its yellowy lines slipped
across each other and slid along the floor.
President Kala picked up the flywhisk
and swooshed it gently through the sunbeams
and the beautiful orange air.

Tell me then, said President Kala,
what characteristics Mourouro, for example,
shares with your heart, what
indispensable parallels you find between
it and your love that you find the need
to appropriate what is not yours and give it away
as a necessary representative of your love?

Imi heard the birds shifting their feathers
on the lawn. The sprinkler had paused.
Other small noises, like the slow shutter,
came forwards to take its place.

Greatness, said Imi. She finished her water
and put the glass down in front of her feet
on the stamped-earth floor.

Another fly arrived and motored around the rim.

Or newly installed underground waterpipes?
said President Kala raising her canary turban.

Busyness, said Imi, leaning forward
to hold her toes in her fingers.

Yellow council buses? Ceaselessness.
Uncle Sidi's Famous Soup Café? Profusion.
Your abstractions apply equally well
to the sea, a flock of birds, the desert sand,
anything, indeed, great, busy and ceaseless.

The brick bridge over the Sorab?
President Kala paused for a moment to light
another cigarette from the Town Hall tin.

Imi stared at the reddening crisscross lines
sliding along the smooth yellow ceiling.

President Kala took a deep drag and continued.
The Yellow Mosque, the Central Post Office,
the shacks in Gaba, the Hotel Faro,
the Museum of Folk Life and Customs,
the eleven music shops, Silek the Painter,
the market square, the new police station,
the fire pump, the telephone exchange,
expensive restaurants, a complaining population,
rubbish in the streets, dust, noise, meanness,
extortion, theft, dangerous driving, rape,
housebreaking, unpaid taxes, perversion,
deception, violence, gangland and murder.

She picked up the flywhisk and stood up.
She towered under the smooth yellow ceiling
like a giant canary. Her sunglasses glistened.
She smoked smokily and thrashed the flywhisk
at the sliding crimson sunbeams.

I wouldn't say that was like love at all.
Your poem, as you please to call it, is banned.

She stamped to the door. The fly in Imi's glass
spiralled slowly into its glassy depths.

This audience is at an end.

President Kala swapped places with
the woman with an elephant gun, who came in.

Imi stood up and touched her hair.
                              Follow me.

The sprinkler suddenly threw itself back into life.
The dry grass dodged and reeled
under each hurled drop. Imi heard
a dog bark far away. And the birds
on the lawn raised their heads, took off,
and circled sleepily into the high sky.

Ao the Kiwi

for Bill Manhire

Ao the kiwi left one night
to find the Happy Hunting Ground.
The moon was shining big and round
and filled the bush with creamy light.

The forecast said there might be showers
in Wedderburn, and heavy dew
in northern parts of Oamaru
and Weston in the early hours.

The outlook was especially bleak
for areas of Tekapo,
where early morning falls of snow
would block the road to Cattle Creek.

Temperatures of one or two
would be the norm round Ikawai;
the outlook being cold and dry,
with freezing fog in Timaru.

Ao turned his beady eyes
towards the moon. He stropped his claws
against a knot of windlestraws
and said his one or two goodbyes.

He left his little tree-root nest
and waddled out towards the creek,
pronging huhus with his beak
along the way, and headed west.

The stories of his family tree
were full of courage, plans and death,
of struggling to your dying breath
to seek out Heaven, and be free –

free from being half-extinct
and lurking in the darkling dark
poking round in bits of bark.
Ao watched the moon and blinked.

Somewhere in the golden dawn,
his father's father always said,
kiwis sunbathed, flew and bred
a million strong on Heaven's lawn.

Packed in like a swarm of men,
a halo hung on every head,
at last they would be saved, he said,
and never have to hide again.

Ao saw a mighty band
thronging in the golden grass:
this, he knew, would come to pass
if he could find the Promised Land.

He flapped his rudimentary wings,
tapped his claws and flexed his knees.
The moon sailed past the clutching trees
and freed itself from earthly things.

What were generations for?
To prime the perfect hero's genes,
so he, by their developed means,
might make the world to come secure.

And now amidst the moonlit roots
he waddled forth upon his quest,
leaving youth's abstracted nest
for more responsible pursuits.

I won't list all the things he took
in case you fall asleep – like slugs,
a pouch of crispy huhu bugs,
a hat, a scarf, a map, a book,

a glow-worm lantern, sun-protector,
jandals made of matai bark,
boots for climbing after dark,
a bag of worms, a rear reflector,

beak-cream, claw-file, rope, galoshes,
tins of scroggin, puttees, tea,
a set of folding cutlery,
two two-sided macintoshes,

thermos, tissues, glucose bars,
freeze-dried wasps, a spade, an axe,
a tube of waterproofing wax,
a water-purifier, jars

of Weta Paste (Superior Mix),
a small sombrero for the sun,
twenty good-luck cards, a gun,
a set of lightweight walking-sticks,

and two small skis. The bright moon shone
like someone's finger through the bush.
He hupped his pack. The gentle swoosh
of pines and piupius waved him on.

But just before he left, he stood
and thought of all the heroes' quests
before him: all the tales, the tests,
the brave, the true, the right, the good,

the farewells, struggles, welcomes, tears,
the dangers, damage, dreams and dares,
the hopes and nightmares, cheers and scares,
the fights, the follies, foes and fears

etcetera. The slow moon sailed
amongst the stars. He clicked his beak.
He took two steps towards the creek
and stopped. The kowhai crowns were veiled

with dabs of snow. The whekis quivered.
Far away the hills turned blue
and glittered cold. A kea flew
across the moonbeam. Ao shivered.

Heroes who had gone before
had not returned, or never found
the longed-for Happy Hunting Ground.
He closed his little eyes. He saw

Hapopo, Rona, Hina, Iwi,
Pa and Tutaua, whose stories
pictured all their fatal glories –
heroes every little kiwi

knew by heart and soul. He thought
of death by sunlight, death by water,
death by man, the angry slaughter
disappointed spirits brought

on those that crossed them; snow and rivers,
waterfalls and grasping roots,
lightning, thunder, guns and boots,
coughs and sneezes, flushes, shivers,

flu and footrot, wonky wings,
plain exhaustion, broken claws,
blindness, deafness, baldness, sores,
corns, exposure, sunburn, stings,

and all the various diseases
known to kiwis. Humpf, he said.
Let's go. He hupped his little head
and started – heart attacks and wheezes,

freezing, burning, madness, shocks,
feather-droop, hallucinations –
stop! Whatever dark privations
lay in wait, whatever knocks,

whatever trials, whatever tests,
he'd see them through. So Ao tramped
across the ferny clearing, stamped
around his family's family nests

and struck across the ponga flat
against a gentle, freezing wind
and flapping piupius, grim, determined,
overloaded, pitapat

over a barky, icy mound –
and there, before the first tawhais,
he saw before his very eyes
the shining Happy Hunting Ground!

The lawns were packed with kiwi brothers,
just like all the stories said.
Ao scratched his little head
and waddled back to tell the others.

The Tale of Lawrence of Arabia post mortem

Made by stabbing pins while under the influence of nicotine at the automatic writings of T.E.Lawrence as recorded by Jane Sherwood (British Library Ref. TESh1959385/6786544.45/34556/prb/JSHL/12.234567012234455432 22.16)

darkness rent
with interludes
but having flickered
I could no longer
fumbled
in the dimness
a ribbon of boys
on bicycles meadows
I thought
hedges and trees
where I came upon
a convenient and
rested my nakedness
finding a shop where
ready-made garments
were a very
unhappy region in the
physical way

I know only
too well
the volcano had
disappeared but
a young man
from which a
wide area of glowing
is hardly possible
in this place
jumped the gap
between us like
an electric spark
by such means

horrid emanations
in spite of
setbacks of the promise

a good deal
of suffering now
the agony
the lucidity
the new vigour
so perhaps
red–hot pincers
is already
some years
and the drop
we shall attain
must be

naturally we started
from a higher
there are
ships here
the desert has all
so thinking
I had climbed
another set
of inexorables
so as not
to get hurt
muddy colour
pleasant
nor to feel
I cultivated what
goes wrong on earth
divided in space
whatever light
too intense
so each must
and stay

I begin now
it is a vast
maybe warped
solitude and savour
too blind and weak
and around the issue
yet a fever
of impatience
unless I bludgeon
the books
I could make here
clean clear lovely
an exact replica
of it and
for as long
or short a time
whichever
manifestation of
a riper
so here I am
but that I know
I should be
this sheer
never know

to whom
I am
strongly therefore
fascinate me
my old habit
is a fluid state
in the flesh
print bind and tool
even as
he cannot easily
bear the higher
conditions and
withdrew it so
that his illumination
broke the silence

we agreed to
not to be
I can see now
to love or
to risk all
I could
value apart from
to each and all
I failed
so lamentably

a stream
of pure joy
us mere receptors
this and much more
I suppose
paid for by
the upshot many
lives paid poisoned all
this and that
I did I
bear on my own
body will
exonerate me
our work here
is a I need
to be far more
let me try
fail his tests
another outcome
immense ages
there is only
as we are
this is the crux
of the mystery
the past
unrolls for me
the framework
of beauty to
his youthful years

clearly divine
plan I can see
so know it
a certainty
so I for one
see clearly stranger
forms this
great end
what is
it makes no sense

some of my
friends from
being a mere
there is a quiet glow
at times he grasps
quietly and sanely
into which
at first and
his charming wife
I remember
the hazards
one can better
and hope in the lost
I suppose one may
be a
too-common problem
there are few
and were loath
to leave him
the agony of
tedious to describe
remain in coma
this is where
will be among us
all behind

I may seem
grass trees and flowers
true I do not want

or any particular
or perhaps
it would be mere
to explain how
and a good
deal of travelling
for instance
there is certainly
so we are intensely
among those who
am I orientated
since one
wonders whether
who have their
lives and ignored without
speculating upon
its ascent and
its probable return
I watch all this
the mere
the conditions
the further
the known facts
the chaotic
the guarantee
the love
the Absolute
a better
lesser gods
a more limited
ground
of all
being
finally
spirit

there
have been
adequate
but since
not yet

The Ferret of Shalott

Part 1

On either side the M1 lie
Long lines of towerblocks, bright and high,
That crowd the earth and poke the sky,
And through their feet the road runs by
　　　To much-more tower'd Raddlescott.
And up and down the lorries go,
Gazing where the chimneys blow
Round a new-town there below,
　　　The new-town of Shalott.

Washing darkens, windows quiver,
Little breezes cough and shiver
Through the cars that run forever
By the new-town like a river,
　　　Flowing down to Raddlescott.
Four glass walls and four glass towers
Overlook a pot of flowers,
And the shaking flat embowers
　　　The Ferret of Shalott.

By his window, near the road,
Roar the red containers, tow'd
By straining trucks: and freight and load,
Bus and van and taxi flow'd,
　　　Snarling down to Raddlescott.
But who hath seen him wave his hand?
Or at the window seen him stand?
Or is he known in all the land,
　　　The Ferret of Shalott?

Only postmen, posting early,
In amongst the carparks daily,
Hear a song that echoes barely
From the towerblock, winding sparely
　　　Down to tower'd Raddlescott.

And by the moon the policeman weary,
Plodding in the shadows airy,
Listening, whispers, "Tis the scary
    Ferret of Shalott.'

Part 2

There he plays by night and day
Computer games in colours gay.
He has heard a whisper say
A curse is on him if he stay
    To look down to Raddlescott.
He knows not what the curse may be,
And so he playeth steadily,
And little other care hath he,
    The Ferret of Shalott.

And moving through a TV clear
That stands before him all the year,
Shadows of the world appear.
There he sees the M1 near
    Roaring down to Raddlescott.
There the traffic's eddy whirls,
And there the choking diesel-swirls
And the slowly stalking girls
    Pass onward from Shalott.

Sometimes a bunch of rowdies glad,
A shivering drunk, unsure and sad,
Sometimes a shiny lager-lad
Or long-haired girl in black boots clad
    Goes by to tower'd Raddlescott.
And sometimes in the TV blue
The ladettes stagger two by two.
He hath no pretty girl and true,
    The Ferret of Shalott.

But in his game he still delights
To imitate the magic sights,

For often through the howling nights
A funeral, with screams and lights
    And music, went to Raddlescott.
Or when the moon was overhead,
Came two young lovers, lately wed;
'I am half sick of shadows,' said
    The Ferret of Shalott.

Part 3

A stone's-throw from his dingy wall,
She rode out of the shopping mall:
The sun shone on her carryall
And flashed upon the bicycle
    Of sweet Forget-Me-Not.
Saint Christopher discretely lay
Upon her bright décolleté
And sparkled as she biked her way
    Beside obscure Shalott.

The Raleigh emblem glittered free,
Like to some shape of stars we see
Hung in the endless Galaxy.
The silver spokes spun merrily
    As she rode down to Raddlescott.
And from her arms two bracelets hung,
A shining stud shone in her tongue,
And as she rode her earrings rung
    Beside remote Shalott.

All in the blue and smoky weather
Smoothly shone the saddle-leather;
The hair-grip and the hair-grip feather
Fluttered like a flame together
    As she rode down to Raddlescott;
As often through the shrouded night
Below the starry clusters bright
Some shining meteor, trailing light,
    Moves over still Shalott.

Her high, clear brow in sunlight glow'd,
In burnished blurs the pedals trode,
From underneath her helmet flow'd
Her icecream curls as on she rode,
　　　As she rode down to Raddlescott.
And from the bins and from the green
She flashed across the TV screen.
'Tirra lira,' by the green
　　　Sang Forget-Me-Not.

He left the game, he left his chair,
He made three paces down the stairs,
He saw bright windows everywhere,
He saw her waving, icecream hair –
　　　He looked down to Raddlescott.
Out flew the games and floated wide,
The TV cracked from side to side:
'The curse is come upon me,' cried
　　　The Ferret of Shalott.

Part 4

In the stormy east-wind straining,
The teeming car tail-lights were waning,
The canal in its banks complaining,
Drearily the low sky raining
　　　Over tower'd Raddlescott.
Down he came and found a car
Abandoned by the lightless Spar,
And sprayed across the bumper bar
　　　da Ferret of Shalott.

Lying, dressed in tracksuit white
That loosely flapped to left and right –
The rain upon him falling light –
Through the noises of the night
　　　He glided down to Raddlescott.
And as the headlights veered along
The yellow-lighted streets among,

They heard him singing his last song,
　　The Ferret of Shalott.

Heard a sad song, dark, unholy,
Chanted loudly, chanted lowly,
Till his blood was frozen slowly
And his eyes were darken'd wholly,
　　Turn'd to tower'd Raddlescott.
For ere he reached, upon his ride,
The first house by the canal-side,
Singing in his song he died,
　　The Ferret of Shalott.

Under tower and balcony,
By walkway and by gallery,
A gleaming shape he glided by,
Dead-pale between the houses high,
　　Silent into Raddlescott.
Along the precinct out they came,
Holding high their lighter-flames
And round the car they read his name,
　　da Ferret of Shalott.

Who is this? And what is here?
And in the bright apartment near
Died the sound of party cheer
And they hugged themselves for fear,
　　All the girls of Raddlescott.
Forget-Me-Not mused a little space.
She said, 'He has a lovely face.
God in his mercy lend him grace,
　　The Ferret of Shalott.'

Rabies!

A true story

1   A decision on a day off

I woke up, got up, and walked purposefully towards the
Council Bus Depot. It was a warm, white day and the streets
were puddled with last night's rain. The city walls were perfectly
black. The statue of Atatürk looked especially big in the
morning light. I read the Bus Information for a while, but
couldn't decide what to do. I waited on the pavement, hoping
that something would move me to choose where to go for some
unaccountable reason. I stood in a puddle as the morning got
warmer and whiter. Nothing happened. I splashed back to the
Institute and looked at my map. I changed my shoes and had
some tea and decided, eventually, to go to Ergani.

It comforts me now that I did not climb, at first, on the Ergani
bus on some happy impulse which I might have mistaken for my
own unconscious heart. I had seen the town before, from the
bus to Elazig, a month before and remembered now that I had
liked the look of it and the greenbrown hill behind it. There
was nothing, then, very deep in my choice: the events that were
about to unfold can, therefore, be put down on the roll of acci-
dent and chance.

2   Ergani and its greenbrown hill

I got off the bus and walked purposefully through the small
streets of Ergani until I reached the back of the town, which lay
at the foot of the greenbrown hill. It was warm and the ground
was puddled with last night's rain. The hot air, heavy with
liquid, drew the plants, grass and blossom into their fullest
ripeness, in which they shone like wax. The tarmac road ended
and became a path scooped out by cartwheels. Men on horse-
back galloped, muted by long grass, into the fields on either side
of me. I began to climb the hill.

The long, zigzag path was cut through bright brown earth and neatly lined with stones. In faroff fields that climbed the hillsides, shepherds sat on rocks amongst their sheep. I could see the shoulders of their capes swinging gently to and fro like the wings of aeroplanes.

The morning got warmer. I continued to zig and then zag. Above me, the top of the hill burst into a cold explosion of sharp rocks. Below, the greenbrown slopes ran away into a glistening flatness. The long, straight road back to Diyarbakir lay along it like a scratch scored in wood.

3 The shepherds and their sheep

I stopped. The wind blew the cherry blossom below me. It frothed. I saw three shepherds with their dogs purposefully driving flocks of sheep along the hillsides, each invisible to the other, each in a different direction. I hurried on and soon reached the top.

4 The man in the mosque

The wind squealed through a patch of scrubby bushes. I could have touched the clouds racing over my head. Piles of snow rattled like nails in the hollows. The Diyarbakir road, now in sunshine, gleamed like a chrome-yellow ribbon.

A small mosque lay low in the shelter of a stone wall. Beside it, a spiky tree with coloured rags for leaves shook and snapped in the wind. I went carefully closer. A man was crouched in the porch. I stopped. He was wearing a knitted beanie and a white flannel shirt. He looked at me. I stayed where I was. He manipulated his galoshes. I couldn't decide if his manner was normal. I bowed.

He flapped a hand at me. The rags cracked like fireworks on the spiky tree. I tiptoed from stone to stone to the porch. He took my hand as a matter of course. I couldn't help noticing that his ears were red and worried. He led me inside.

In an outer room something lay on the floor wrapped completely in a blanket. The noise of the wind and the rags ran out. We walked purposefully into the inner rooms. They were green and dark. Green windowpanes let in a little wobbly light. The building shook. He took off his shoes: therefore, so did I. We walked into the innermost room. The windowpanes here were yellow. His ears gleamed. Plastic lamps hung from the ceiling on bits of string. The lights were small and still.

We stood in front of a green, green-embroidered curtain. The man pulled the curtain back. In the wall was a metal grille. Behind it reared a piece of pink and turquoise cloth, glittering darkly with sequins. The man pushed me towards it. I was surprised at his violent manners.

5   Shame

I goggled at the cloth. What a shame. Although it might only take a second, to express veneration was beyond me. I had none of the signs. I shrank from guessing. I stood still, aware that my confusion, the longer it lasted, might be taken for defiance. The lamps swung in circles, carrying their yellow lights. They seemed happy. I had trespassed without care. For a while, this pleased me. As I grew more desperate, it pained me that while I had learned to be less of one thing, I had failed to become more of another.

I put on a look of serviceable humility. Perhaps it seemed rude. He pushed me out. He pulled his beanie over his ears. I put on my shoes anyhow. We stood in the porch. The rags snapped. The man directed me to the grey edge of the hilltop instead. I stumbled away purposefully, not to satisfy his judgement of me as a man who had mistaken his soul, but to escape from an affair that intimated that although I may somewhere have had a soul, I didn't know where it was.

6   A monastery

The ruins stuck up from the foundations of the highest rocks.
Ergani looked pale and distinct, way below. I felt cold and sick.
The wind, unable to move this tangle of boulders, buffeted me on
purpose. We nearly came to blows. Suddenly, I was standing on a
gleaming stone toilet seat. Its beautifully polished rim shone at the
sky. All their arses were bones. I clattered down over the ridge. I
reached the zigzag path. Rain shot out of the clouds. Now the
world was moving. I stopped in a puddle. The rain rapped into it
like gravel. I took a deep breath. Then I started purposefully down.

7   Dogs one

In the quiet of my breather, on a zig of the greenbrown hillside, I
had listened to my heart. But only its beating, which was literal.
Now, as I jumped down the hill in the rain, it couldn't be heard
above the woundup world. So I stopped again, in case it wanted to
tell me something else. It didn't get the chance.

At first, I thought it was the rain rattling through some scrubby
bush. It might have been the echo of stones bursting out from my
feet. It might have been the first crackle of thunder. The clouds
began to stand up. The sun looked through. It might have been a
horse scrambling purposefully up the scree. It might have been
snakes going home. It might have been the cherry blossom boiling
over. But it was dogs.

8   Only a tree

They pattered purposefully up, still out of sight, the hillside below
me. I began to cry and talk. Whatever monsters breasted the little
stony brown horizon, they might be disarmed with tears or
persuaded by reason. It wasn't what I called me that threw up these
defences. It was something saving itself. I didn't know it. I am only
a tree on the mountain of me.

9 Dogs two

Three white dogs swarmed up onto the zag. They tiptoed between
the puddles. Their mouths were winched open. Their gums were
shocking pink. Their tongues were glossed with saliva, which
drooled over. The clouds drew up into cones. Sunshine shot down
the sides and shimmered on the tiny drops at the end of each
doghair. The dogs stood still, like glass freaks. The wind darted
hither and thither, then threw itself round the hillside. This
arrangement lasted a minute or two. Having looked at them first in
the face, as I would a new friend, I looked further. They wore
metal collars, out of which stuck a crown of metal spikes. My hair
stood on end. While there was time, I felt some satisfaction. It's
not every day a dysphemism comes true. They trotted forwards.
The mountain got ready the tree to die by shooting its roots full of
anaesthetic. It would still hurt. They sat down round me.

I said goodbye to the part of me I knew. My surroundings shut up
shop. I stood on a pinhead. At least I was half way to nothing now.
So it might be quick.

The dogs stood up again. One barked, the second dribbled and the
third snapped. By this fairytale round I saw they were a family. We
were drenched in sunshine. Beyond its spotlight, the greenbrown
hillsides looked grey. The dogs scrabbled nearer. My legs shook. As
I reeled like a sapling, they all barked. Screws of spit flew around
like septic glue. One wrapped itself onto my cheek. I raged. I
roared. They strained backwards and howled. Their teeth slid out
of their gums to full length. They yawned like apes. I armed myself
purposefully with my beastliness. No one, after all, wants to be
eaten alive.

10 A bite and a whistle

They snapped at me in a circle limelit by the sun. The dogs turned
canary yellow. I had hopes that such freaks wouldn't ordinarily bite
me. I squared up purposefully to two. I howled at them. The dog
I'd called Dad slavered behind me. I turned round. It didn't work.
He picked his way suddenly between the puddles and injected his

teeth through my thigh. It made the noise of a dropped egg. I swayed like a chopped tree. I faced him. Myself, I was no good. I needed other arms. The divine spark that fires mankind up from the company of dogs lay exactly in those things that were most useless to me now: my intelligence, my humanity and my soul. I bent over for a handful of stones that shone wetly between the puddles. I only touched one.

The wind sent a shiver down the path. I saw it go, like it was cut with a cheesewire. It promised salvation. The clouds climbed themselves away into backbones, their heavy ends, like wrung cloths, dropping rain. The sun glared. The dogs looked close to ignition. They burst over the stones that lined the path and, all orange, melted away.

11   The yellow road home

The truth was more plain. I ran purposefully down to Ergani. I waited half an hour for a bus. Different, flat clouds closed on the sun. When I got back to Diyarbakir, at the end of the yellow road, I sat on my bed at the Institute and read the news with a dictionary. The pages shook. The flue sucked my fire out of the stove into a starry black sky. Don't be disturbed, I worked out, by the bombers. I dreamed a metal wood spilled through the door to my bed. It waited, packed closely round me, while I finished a melon called sleep.

12   Sevtap rings

In the morning, which was warm and white, I was innocent for two seconds. I rolled away from the sunshine in my big window. My trousers, standing from a wire round the stove, looked at me with two astonished eyes, bloodshot round the edges. I stared at them with pity. I'd taken a wound off. I didn't feel my leg.

I got up, got dressed and went out. I bought a wet cheese from a shop across the road. At the end of Ali Emiri 4 the city walls stood up, deckled and black in the sky. The elastic back of my leg tightened. I walked purposefully to the Preparation Room at the Institute. Azize Ipek swayed at her desk and wrote. I said good morning. Fikri Dikmen lay in his chair and looked sideways out the window at the brown rosegarden. Good morning, they said. I sat down tautly. I was on two hot coins. I dropped the cheese on my desk. Did I enjoy my day off. Yes, I said, Ergani was very beautiful. Fikri Dikmen rolled his head and looked at me emptily. Especially the cherry blossom. Azize Ipek smiled with watery kindness. Except, I said, I'd been bitten by a dog on the way down. By a what, said Fikri Dikmen. He sat up and came to a point. Dogs. Fikri Dikmen disappeared through the door, which banged shut. I looked at the roses. Fikri Dikmen shouted. The noise came deflectedly through the window. He is telling Sevtap to ring the hospital, said Azize Ipek, her eyes swimming with excitement. Suddenly, the brightness spilled out. How awful, she whispered.

13   Terror

Fikri Dikmen threw the door open. He was panting. Quick, he said. I got up. The punchholes stretched and hurt. Through the window, sudden rain smacked the brown roses. We ran to the gates. Ali Emiri 4 was buzzing with water. Wait a minute. Fikri Dikmen splashed away for his car. I stood purposefully still in the doorway. I was still well. The rain leapt down the street. The sky quickened. The front garden jostled. Fikri Dikmen's car, like a red fish, glided to the gates.

I was on my way.

The city walls showed up and spilled away while the wipers flapped at the rain. Someone urged a horse between two taxis. We stopped at Fikri Dikmen's house. Lunch, he said, and smiled. We had hamburgers. The windows steamed up. We sat at a red formica table. The hospital could have prescribed lunch. We sat in the livingroom and watched TV. I sat on nails. Fikri Dikmen uncovered his watch. Okay, he said, time to go.

We drove down rivers. The windows steamed up. This is it, said Fikri Dikmen. Quick.

14   State Hospital for Chest and Lung Diseases

The doors were crowded. We barged in. Blue smoke surged round
the ceiling. Fikri Dikmen pushed a line of people away. We ran
past numbered clinics. We stopped in a corridor. Have a cigarette,
he said. Wait here. I turned into a rosegrey window where a man
in a big turban was smoking with a long cigarette holder. We
bowed a little at each other. The hospital garden fell down to the
Dijle. Stick houses hung on the bank. His hand trembled. Our
smokes wandered around together. The wet glass spoiled the view.

Quick, said Fikri Dikmen. We ran upstairs. He was holding a card.
My leg didn't hurt. We ran down an empty corridor and stopped
at a temporary door. This is it, he said. He knocked. While we
waited, he gave me the card. Shoes squeaked on the lino. Darkness
stole along the temporary walls. Come in, said a light voice.

We sat in a wide, white and glassy room like a carpark level. Dr
Nejati Koch sat behind his desk. A plastic rose in a glass vase faded
in the brightness. Good morning, he said. I sat on skewers. I'd seen
him often at the Institute. His white shirt crackled. His brush
moustache rustled. His hair lay like liquorice. Tea's on the way, he
said lightly. Let's look at your leg.

Hobbled in chinos, I stared purposefully across the floe of tiles.
Breath from the doctor's nostrils warmed my ham. I wished he
would never decide. My eyes unfocused. Whiteness flooded in.
Thanks, said Dr Koch. He sat behind his desk. I pulled up my
trousers and sat on swords. His fingers made a wigwam. His face
had a smile and a frown. Fikri Dikmen took out his worrybeads.
They started clacking. The treatment for rabies, said the doctor,
isn't very nice here. He sighed and looked at the floodlit windows.
His porcelain skin beamed. The beads stopped. He picked a stetho-
scope out of a drawer. And there might be side effects. I blanched
further. Would I die of a cure.

Fikri Dikmen started his beads again. Clickclack. Clickclack. Dr
Koch rang his intercom. There might be some serum left at
Pirinjlik, he said. It's less risky. It was greek to me. The intercom
rang back. Hello, said the doctor.

15   Three dark roads

While he talked I clittered my teeth and folded the card. Fikri
Dikmen clacked his beads. Someone brought a tray of tea. Dr
Koch covered the intercom with his hand. Help yourselves, he
said. He listened again. My teaspoon tinkled on the glass. My hand
shook. I watched the sugarcubes burst and fizz. Dr Koch sat back.
He left his tea.

Well, there's a choice, he said lightly. Fikri Dikmen clacked faster.
How did I know. Three dark roads. Begin the treatment. Wait a
couple of days to go to Pirinjlik. Do nothing. Ha ha ha.

16   We ran for the door

Dr Koch stood up. He put his unused teaglass carefully on the tray.
The specialist told me the chances are very small. I gasped. I stood
up. Two lances sucked out of my leg. Fikri Dikmen put his beads
in his pocket. There hasn't been a case of rabies in Diyarbakir for
five years. He picked up the stethoscope. Not one. Fikri Dikmen
grabbed my hand. I'd start the treatment. Dr Koch advanced
purposefully. First, he said, go back to Ergani. Quickly. Find the
dog. Fikri Dikmen started for the door. Thus so did I. Tie it up. If
it doesn't die in three or four days you're safe. Let's go, said Fikri
Dikmen. We rushed out. The walls wobbled like cardboard. The
corridor was empty. We ran down the stairs. We barged through
the crowd at the door. Mud spat at the cars. What do I do if it
dies? But the rain was too noisy.

17   Return to Ergani

We hurled back to Fikri Dikmen's. The red fish swam and popped.
Hang on, said Fikri Dikmen. I meant to. I waited. Someone ran
past the gushed window pushing a glass cart full of nuts. A tilley
lamp shone milkily inside like a mobile shrine. I sobbed. Fikri
Dikmen slammed the door. I got these, he said. Raincoats and
waders. This is Erkan's. He put a Sluggers baseball bat on my lap.
We hurtled purposefully out of Diyarbakir. The road was black.

We jumped the lights. One headlight peered sideways. It lit up holes we didn't need to avoid. I held the bat and cried. Evening came down like ink in the rain. You can't beat these Murat stationwagons, said Fikri Dikmen as we crashed into Ergani.

18   Back on the black hill

Nothing did. We slipped and slapped up the greenbrown hill, hurling bright brown earth at the sky. The neat stones rolled away down the hillside. We lurched round the explosion of sharp rocks and stopped by the ragtree. The car clicked and popped. The ribbons hung heavy and still. No one crouched in the mosque porch. Come on, said Fikri Dikmen. Things darkened. We put on raincoats and waders. Fikri Dikmen made purposefully for the monastery ruins. Why not? I tried to keep my heart slow. I flapped forwards after him. And do everything quickly. From this paradox I sank into muddy obscurity.

Fikri Dikmen looked at the shiny toilet seat. Look at this, he said. I stared over the edge instead. Way below, plains carried the grey road to Diyarbakir into the clouds.

19   Looking for shepherds

Back at the car, Fikri Dikmen took out the Slugger and said right, let's go. What was down there, said Fikri Dikmen, pointing the bat at the zigs and zags. Nothing, I said. Right, said Fikri Dikmen, his hem a little waterfall, let's go this way. We squelched to the opposite hillside and stood at the edge. Yellow and green windowpanes oozed on the back of the mosque. But. Quick, he said. We jumped over. I slid on stones. I ran sideways. My waders buckled and popped. The hillside got greener. The sky blackened. We splashed in meadowy herbage. Have a cigarette, said Fikri Dikmen, holding out a packet. We smoked in the open rain.

I could have been a knight in a symbolic landscape, looking for a revelation that depends on a purity of heart he knows he hasn't got and for which he must rely on someone else.

We sploshed purposefully along the darkening meadow. A tree like bent iron stood on its higher edge. Come on, said Fikri Dikmen. He swung the Slugger. I stopped. Two men crouched under the iron branches. Dogs, said Fikri Dikmen. The shepherds crouched under their aeroplane coats. Their eyes glinted through the flaps. Four dogs were tied to the iron trunk.

20 Sunset

We oozed closer. The dog silhouettes snapped and tugged like cardboard cutouts against a bloodred sky. The coats stayed still. Smokepuffs came out of the flaps. The dogs gaped. I waited behind Fikri Dikmen. The walk had elasticated my scabs. They tingled like sherbert fizz. Fikri Dikmen yelled at the coats. Then he flung a storm of words at them. They turned their doors in my direction. Smoke puffed out. I leaned towards the iron tree. The dogs were black. I turned back into the plashy meadow. I was face to face with the shepherds. We shook hands purposefully. Their eyes glinted. They looked like cartoon triangles, nodding, shuffling and stiff. Don't worry, they said. My teeth chattered. The flat dogs danced in front of the red sunset in their collars of metal thorns.

21 Round and round the hill

The shepherds pointed round the hillside. Fikri Dikmen shouted. We shook hands. I wanted to stay: not me was safe. There's more shepherds, said Fikri Dikmen, splashing off. They've got white dogs. Is that what I said? I went after. My waders wobbled and popped. I must have. Boulders burst out of the slimy hillside. On a rolling edge I saw two triangles running towards us. I stopped. Fikri Dikmen stood purposefully in front of me. He waved the Slugger. The sky was hectic. Four dogs ran out under its curtain. My skin crept. They're brown, said Fikri Dikmen. The shepherds squelched nearer. They stopped to talk. The rain drummed on their coats and their eyes glinted. Fikri Dikmen shouted. They gathered their coats. There's no rabies here, they said. Then they ran on. The dogs bristled behind. The triangles rolled round the hillside and sank, like yachts in a pitched sea. They don't know where they are, said Fikri Dikmen.

We got to the car when the sky was coals and ashes.

22 Dr Shimshek's advice

Shell Company were having tea in the Institute tearoom. Twenty teaglasses twinkled and glittered. Blue smoke surged round the ceiling. Dr Shimshek took me to a corner. The walls were shiny: the neon lights buzzed. I was bitten once, in Adana, he whispered. His big, round, shaved head rolled purposefully towards me. I didn't do anything. He picked my shirtsleeve. Nothing happened. He smiled. His tight white collar held his head up like a golf ball on a tee. His kind black eyes popped at me. When you're frightened of water, he murmured, you've had it. Twenty teaspoons rattled. Tea, said Fikri Dikmen. I grabbed it fearlessly. I made some choppy waves and drank it greedily.

That night I sat by the basin and turned the taps on. I was frightened anyway. How was I supposed to know? I dreamed I chucked myself off a rock like a plane and flew away.

23 The day after the night I was a plane

Morning broke. My teeth were bone dry. Rain pricked the window. I lay fearlessly round my pillow. I washed wildly. At nine o'clock Fikri Dikmen tapped on the window. Come on, he said through the glass. The red fish glided out of Ali Emiri 4. We hissed past Republic Park. The bushes shivered and shone. We parked anyhow at the City Council. Quick, said Fikri Dikmen. We ran purposefully upstairs. Where's the Vet department, he shouted. There, said a woman, pointing with a brush. We barged in.

We sat in front of the vet. Fikri Dikmen clacked his beads. Let me sort this out, said the vet. I thought how mean of death to come through such a little hole.

We drove to the vet's house. It was an ochre villa. Let's take the kids, he said. He ran inside. We sat in the station wagon, which fogged up. I stared at the rain dripping off the iron railings and ivy. I bet he earns a bit, said Fikri Dikmen, staring at the ochre villa. The vet came back, dodging under the ivy. He was carrying gumboots and a spade. A tank barged down the road behind us, its tracks tangled in barbedwire and squashed oranges. The ground rumbled. The kids had bows and arrows and a football. I sat between them while we hurtled into Ergani. The arrows were sharp.

24   Return to Ergani again

We skidded up by a pink shed. The Ergani vet walked down the steps swishing a striped walkingstick. Morning, he yelled, bowing brightly on the bottom step. His white suit shone. He peered through the back window. He took out a small notebook. The cover was spotted with damp. He squashed in the back.

Fikri Dikmen gushed us up the greenbrown hill. It was kind of grey. We went up packed tight like a box of good souls killed in a crash down below and going to heaven holding the rubbish with which death had surprised us.

It was cold on top. The vet put his small notebook away. We looked all round. The hillsides were grey. The road to Diyarbakir lay like dirty silver. The vet took his kids to see the mosque. The porch was empty. The stone wall dripped. The door was locked. The prickly tree scratched the sky and wrapped it with rags. Who cares?

We slithered back to the shed. The vet shouted at Fikri Dikmen. The ball baffed our feet. What use was that? I rested in the arms of half a sleep. I sat up suddenly. The Ergani vet smiled. His white suit beamed. The hill of me was sick. The tree next.

25   The house of Arif Finjan

The vet wrote quickly in his small notebook. I watched tiredly.
The pink shed breathed. He wrote more. I swayed a bit. He passed
to page two. Whywhywhy, he said. No one's been up there for
years. He smiled. My mouth started. Whoa, he yelled. He stood
up. His chair screamed away. He swished his striped walkingstick.
He yanked the door. He danced down the steps. He charged the
little meadow. The kids hung out. We craned over. The vet
splashed over the plashy meadow. He yelled. A man was marching
towards town, pulling a squiggle of smoke behind him. The vet
splashed closer. He yelled. The man stopped. The vet took him by
the shoulders and shook him. We peered hopefully. The man's cap
went askew. He held his cigarette out of harm's way. The vet
smiled. He pushed the man away. The man marched off towards
town. We held our breaths. The vet splashed back. The shepherd's
name, he puffed brightly, is Arif Finjan.

We marched to the house of Arif Finjan. First the vet with a small,
damp notebook. Then the vet with a spade on his shoulder. Then
the kids with bows and arrows. Then Fikri Dikmen with the foot-
ball. Then me with rabies, like a baggagetrain about to be picked
off at the back of a shiny army.

26   Someone else's house

Arif Finjan's house seeped. The mud bricks sagged like full
sponges. The shoring sticks bowed. I gasped. Three dogs snored in
the yard, white and brown. The vet slapped the door. Arif Finjan
stared at us. The vet shouted at him. A woundup scarf stood on his
head. His shalvar snapped like sails. He marched off and we went
after. I stamped in puddles fearlessly. I was healthy and sick to
death. We stopped. He, said Arif Finjan, has got three white dogs.
The vet smacked the door. Don't worry, he said to me while we
waited. Cheerio, said Arif Finjan.

27   He's out

A woman stared at us. The vet yelled at her, shaking whitely. He's out, she said. The vet wrote quickly on his small notebook. Her eyes glinted. They're safe anyway, she said. The vet shouted. Some chickens rallied to her jelly boots. The vet turned a page and wrote more. I swayed a bit. They're safe, she said. Two kids with shaved heads stood round her legs. Were they white? My wrinkled brain knew no more. She glared at the notebook. The vet wrote more. The wind ruffled the chickens. Her jelly boots gleamed. The vet crammed two little pages into her hands. We stamped out of the yard and splashed across the plashy meadow. Right, said the vet smiling brightly, we'll wait in my office.

My heart misgave. To wait for someone who didn't want to come.

28   Waiting in a way

We marched Ergani's muddy streets. What's the point? The vet sprang into every restaurant. He looked round carefully. He came out, swishing his striped walkingstick. We splashed on. He leapt into every teahouse. He looked round carefully. Twenty teaglasses twinkled and glittered. Blue smoke surged round the ceiling. Rain drizzled. We came to The Four Brothers Eggs A Speciality. The vet looked round carefully. He marched to a formica table. Where's your brother, he yelled. The shepherd's brother put down his tea and clacked his beads. Fikri Dikmen brought me tea. I sucked it fearlessly. Rain pattered on the roof. The sugar swirled. The shepherd's brother went back to his eggs. We marched out. When he finds him, said the vet, smiling, he'll come. We'll sort it out, said the vet. Have a cigarette, said Fikri Dikmen.

We splashed to Uncle Remzi's. The vet unshouldered his spade. I'm hungry, he said. We marched in. Nice bread here, said the Ergani vet. It was fluffy and yellow. I ate a bit of chicken while I died. There were dots of blood inside.

29   The right shepherd

We stood about in the pink shed for five minutes. The little window fogged up. Then someone stamped up the steps. Knockknock. The vet smiled brightly. There you go, he said. He yanked the door.

The shepherd's eyes glinted. A woundup scarf stood on his head. Give us a moment, said the vet, smiling. The shepherd marched in and we marched out. We heard the vet yelling. We wandered apart on the plashy meadow. The kids shot in the drizzle. Fikri Dikmen clacked his beads. The vet picked his teeth. The sky rolled greyly like a rolling weight.

They're his, yelled his vet in the doorway. He waved his walking-stick and smiled. The cloud opened. Swords of sunlight cut through here and there. That is, I thought they did. The vet called us back. We stood together in the pink shed. I shook hands with the shepherd. I cried. What use was that?

The shepherd stood by the vet's desk and unwound his woundup scarf. The vet yelled. He wrote quickly in his small notebook. He wrote more. We watched in a tired huddle. Rain pricked the roof. I listened fearlessly. Sign this, said the vet. The shepherd wrote slowly on the notebook. Good, said the vet. Now you. I swayed a bit and wrote my name. I leaned on the desk. The vet leaned towards me. He heard you yelling, he whispered, up there and whistled. Thank God, I said.

I bowed at the shepherd. Don't worry, he said. I went outside. The grass was wet and very green. The sky still rolled. Later, we drove back to Diyarbakir along dirty silver.

30   Looking for a cure for death

I started to shake like boiling water. Fikri Dikmen brought tea into the tearoom. My glass tinkled shakily. Cheer up, said Fikri Dikmen. The phone rang. Dr Shimshek, he said, for you. I told him what I thought we'd done. Ah nothing then, said Dr

Shimshek. He sounded angry. Are the dogs tied up? Fikri Dikmen took the phone. I cried. He said uh-huh while he smoked. He said it again. Gazi Street, he said. Uh-huh. I waited purposefully. Uh-huh. Why. Quick, said Fikri Dikmen. Let's go.

We ran into Ali Emiri 4. The red fish glided away. Waterbeads raced down the windows. The city walls showed and slipped away wet black. A horse reared past the window. And a jacket with a machinegun, very close. Quick, said Fikri Dikmen. We ran up some yellow stairs. Dr Öztürk, said the door. A black sofa like a large cat occupied the landing. Fikri Dikmen knocked loudly. Nothing happened. I thought something else would. The cleaner opened the door. He's gone home, she said. Fikri Dikmen ran to the phone. There's no vaccine here, said Fikri Dikmen. Come on. We ran downstairs. Rain pittered on the car roof. I curled up on the leather.

We stopped at Fikri Dikmen's house. I sat in the livingroom and watched TV. Fikri Dikmen whispered down the phone. There's no vaccine, he said. I listened sideways. He took out his worry-beads. Or at the Air Base. They ran out last week. I watched a pink cartoon. That they had run out was bad. That they had cause was awful. I stood up purposefully. Quick, said Fikri Dikmen and I together. We glided back to the Institute. The windows fogged up. A camel trotted the other way, loaded with wet sacks. Dr Shimshek waved angrily from his car. We got out and got in.

31   Return to Ergani again again

We walloped away. The black Mercedes thuddered like an aeroplane in the bluster. Evening shades ran down the sky like ink. The greenblack hill breathed its shape up on a lemon craze. I pressed my nose purposefully on the window. I'll never believe it's the end. We crashed into Ergani.

Shades spilled over us slowly. Dr Shimshek threaded his black Mercedes up and down the small streets of Ergani. Mud spilled out of stone walls. I watched through the window. Puddles leapt out. The gears ground their teeth. I bounced on the leather. The wingmirrors scraped and flabbered along the walls. Dr Shimshek turned on the lights. Mud, stone and bright wet black. I saw a fire in a window. I saw a candle. A lamp held a yellow arm out in the rain, which glittered. We leapt a clod of wet bricks. I saw a yard floundering with peelings. I didn't shake. I was a fearless passenger.

32 Dr Shimshek knocks

We stopped. Dr Shimshek squeezed out of the black Mercedes and banged on a door. Then another. He loomed at my window. His big, shaved head rolled towards me. He's out, said Dr Shimshek. His tight white collar gleamed. So's his sons. His kind black eyes popped. So's the dogs. My head kind of blurred. He got in. The foam sighed. We'll wait, he said kindly.

We waited. Darkness dropped everywhere. The sky was dirty silver. Rain pattered on the roof. The walls spilled brown water. The windows fogged up. I saw a lamp lighting an eiderdown. I waited purposefully. I was still well.

I looked at my face in the window. It looked small and pinched. Me and my face leaned together. Our nose flattened whitely. I looked at my eyes. Rained glittered at them. My hair was cut by the night. Big ears stuck out sideways. I leapt back. Someone else was stuck on the window. Death raced round me. It was lit with a lighter. Someone else's white nose stuck to the window like a glo-worm. The light flibbled at me. The face vanished.

We waited. Dr Shimshek's big, shaved head watched and turned. I curled up. Aha! said Dr Shimshek. It was him.

33 Sitting in the dark

Dr Shimshek squeezed out of the car. The shepherd splashed past under his aeroplane coat. His eyes glinted through the flaps. Dr Shimshek splashed through the muddy rubble. The shepherd stamped inside. Dr Shimshek ran after him to his door. He yanked it open. His big, shaved head lit up like the moon. He shouted.

The shepherd stamped and yelled. Dr Shimshek marched splashily back to the black Mercedes.

They're still out, said Dr Shimshek, puffing. His tight white collar gleamed. He got in. No one told them to tie them up. He sounded angry. Well, he wouldn't do it anyway. His big head turned. He says they're safe. We'll wait, he said. The door shut. Darkness sat with us and we waited. Aha! said Dr Shimshek. It was them.

34 The shepherd's sons

The shepherd's sons splashed past under their aeroplane coats. The dogs splattered after. Night put its arms round them. They stamped inside and were gone. Dr Shimshek squeezed out of the car. The dogs sat lapping in the yard. The arm of light from the lamp reached out and glittered. Were they white? This time, Dr Shimshek knocked. Nothing happened. I thought something else would. I waited purposefully.

The door opened.

The shepherd's sons stood like black cards against the lamplight. Dr Shimshek's collar gleamed like a bird. Dr Shimshek yelled. I wiped the window. Dr Shimshek reached into the doorway and grabbed the shepherd's sons. He pulled them down the steps. Drops shot off their coats. In a sky of sprayed stars they stumbled into the yard. Don't, I said. I watched Dr Shimshek shake his hands at the dogs. The shepherd's sons picked up the dogs' ropes. They stood like grey cards against the spilling brown wall. The dogs gleamed like glass here and there. Were they white? Sphered in water, I looked fearlessly at what I never remembered. Dr Shimshek pushed the shepherd's sons back up to the wall. The dogs gleamed. Dr Shimshek turned. His big, shaved head glowed like the moon. He splashed back to the car. He looked angry. He got in. The foam sighed.

35 Betrayal

He switched on the headlights. The shepherd's sons put their arms
over their eyes. A plate of white light threw itself at them and
stuck on the wall, spilling and shining. Is that them? said Dr
Shimshek kindly. My lips parted slowly. Dr Shimshek started the
car. The shapes flattened on the wall, run all over by spilling water.
Dr Shimshek took off the handbrake. I shut my eyes.

The black Mercedes hissed and joggled forwards. Wet bricks
lumped and crumbled under it. Puddles leapt out. The black
Mercedes stopped. I looked out. At the end of the bonnet, white
as the light, the shepherd's sons gleamed and glittered with their
dogs. Drained of movement and colour, they stood stiffly at the
wall, flattened with brightness. Their eyes glinted. The dogs
sparkled. I looked away. The black Mercedes glared. Which one
bit you? said Dr Shimshek. He turned.

I couldn't remember, so I had no doubts. The small dog, gleaming
and shivering like glass under pressure, yawned like an ape. Prickles
pricked my skin from inside. The little one, I whispered. On fire
with shame, I curled up on the leather and shut my eyes again.

36 Arif Finjan's sons

Good, said Dr Shimshek. It bites everyone. A bird lifted my
stomach. But no one has died, said Dr Shimshek.

He rammed the black Mercedes into reverse. It hissed and joggled
over the crumbled bricks. Stones pinged away and splashed in the
mud. We crashed away. Dr Shimshek puffed. The windows fogged
up.

The wingmirrors scraped and flabbled down a steep, narrow street.
I saw a fire in a window. I saw a candle. Rain spilled out of the
grey stone walls. We stopped in a puddle at the house of Arif
Finjan. Dr Shimshek yanked the handbrake. He squeezed out of
the black Mercedes and splashed to the door and stamped up the
steps. Don't, I said. The rain shrank to a glittery mist that didn't

fall. It hung in the black night like sprayed stars. Dr Shimshek knocked.

The door opened.

Arif Finjan's sons stood like paper cards against a sickly paraffin light. The light swung and the shapes, huge in shalvars, slipped and squeezed yellowly. A pile of brown blankets swung brown shadows on the floor. A tin plate skimmed off the table and returned, again and again. I slumped on the leather. Dr Shimshek reached into the doorway and grabbed the sons of Arif Finjan. He yelled and pulled them down the steps. A huge dog stirred in the mud. I watched Dr Shimshek shake his hands at the dog. Arif Finjan's sons picked up its rope. Dr Shimshek pushed them towards the white plate of light.

37   Two out of three

Drops flew off them. They stumbled in explosions of tiny stars. The unfalling rain hung and shifted where they stumbled like a huge bead curtain. They crashed into the light. Their eyes glinted. Their thin moustaches threw shadows like knives. I leaned forward. The huge white dog burst into light like it had been switched on. Prickles pricked my skin from inside. It yawned like an ape. It strained backwards and howled. Its teeth slid out of its gums to full length.

I nodded purposefully at Dr Shimshek. On fire with shame, I turned to look at the lightpinned sons of Arif Finjan. Their arms were over their eyes. I started to cry.

I had lost the strings that tied the cause and effect of my life to the processes of knowledge. I had no idea what this scene meant. I only knew it reminded me of something I'd forgotten that carried with it, unaccountably, melancholy, shame and betrayal. I thought it might be the effect of rabid poison that, to blunt the fear of death and its pain, was moving me into a world of inconsequent imaginings. What evolution that would have been.

Dr Shimshek splashed back to the black Mercedes. He got in. Good, he said kindly. It's got a vaccination certificate. We crashed out of Ergani. Night put its arms round us.

38   One dark road home

We roared home. The lights of Diyarbakir shone in towers of flats. Dr Shimshek turned his big, shaved head. Start the treatment, he said kindly. Now. I was still well. The third dog looked like the others. A shadow cut out of a plate of light. We rattled into Diyarbakir. A tank went past the other way, pulling a train of barbed wire and squashed vegetables. I leaned forwards on the leather. What's the side effects? I said. Dr Shimshek didn't turn. His big, shaved head sat like a moon in the sky of the windscreen. Brain damage, he said. We joggled and splashed through the blackly wet city walls. I felt like a hand closed round me. And death, said Dr Shimshek. The rain had shrunk into a curtain of stars.

39   Saving the mountain, saving the tree

Fikri Dikmen was waiting in the tearoom. Have a cigarette, he said. He clacked his beads. There wasn't any tea. The clean teaglasses stood upsidedown in rows, glinting on the counter. What happened? he said. Dr Shimshek told him. Fikri Dikmen laid his hand on mine. I recognized his kindness. Maybe that was a step on the way to the recovery of my too selfish soul. The body might follow. If it didn't, at least it proved I had a soul. So death was kind of relative. Dr Shimshek finished the story.

We walked purposefully to Fikri Dikmen's house. We sat at the red formica table and had cheese on toast. Dr Shimshek drove away. I'll be back tomorrow, he said.

I limped home. Ali Emiri 4 was empty. Scaffolding up on the new block of flats next door creaked gently. Two redstained boiled eggs sat in the crumbly mud like roc droppings. Down at the end, the city walls clutched at the carpark like a huge fist hanging on to the edge of the world.

I lay on my bed shaking. The stove shook. I left the light on. If there had been a powercut I would have followed it.

40 Resolution

So I submitted to a treatment that could kill me for a complaint I mightn't have.

41 Thank God it's open

I gave up thinking. I curled up in a mattress stuffed with something like faith.

It was a warm, white day. The streets were puddled with last night's rain. The red fish swam to the Institute gates. Pale, white sunshine played with the heads of Fikri Dikmen, Dr Shimshek, the vet, and his cousin from Gaziantep. I squashed in. The windows fogged up. Hello, we all said. We bounced through the city walls. They were black and glistened. Did they all worry? We skidded to a stop at the Health Centre. It sat in front of the State Hospital like a joey in mum's pocket. Fikri Dikmen rubbed the windscreen. Thank God it's open, he said. So I did.

We got out and went in. Six buckets of sand stood by the door. Over the door were a pick and shovel crossed. Probably the labour of medicine. We all marched into a little anteroom. We waited tightly together. Dr Shimshek smiled. My feelings were so complicated they cancelled each other out. A doctor and a nurse came in the front door. Hello, we all said. Dr Shimshek whispered to the nurse. The doctor shook my hand. How's the kids? he said to the vet. Fikri Dikmen clacked his beads. The nurse opened a door.

42 The nurse

The room was yellow. The doctor closed the door. The nurse frowned. As bad as an alarmed pilot. Lie down, said the doctor. A big red leather couch aahed like a mouth. I got in and shut my eyes. I don't care about pain; I just hate its business.

43   Injection no. 1

Pull up your shirt, said the doctor. So I did. I rolled my head away. Are you taking, said the doctor, who had changed sides, anything else? No. I opened my eyes. I was deceived. The nurse was holding up a little hypodermic. It was full of milky liquid. I smiled.

I watched as the needlepoint pricked my stomach. As if it was looking for a splinter. Then it slid in. I gasped. I felt it spike what was in its way as it went in. All mine. All alive. It stopped as if it was resting and looking round in the reddish dark. The nurse pressed the little plunger. In the right half of my stomach, like an alien's penis, it ejaculated milk, whose effect was beyond me.

The milk spread away. All I had to do was wait and see what happened. The questing wire slid out. The nurse dropped it in a bin. Would my brain be able to communicate brain damage if it was damaged? That's less terrible. I sat up. I shook hands with the doctor. The nurse bowed. Get well soon, they said.

44   Home to bed

No drink now, said Dr Shimshek and smiled. And keep warm. The red fish rattled through the black city walls. A soldier bowled two tyres through puddles in the carpark. Now I had no purpose. Someone tapped the window with a stook of striped walkingsticks. The sun smiled waterily. Something imperceptible ran through the hill of me. The tree waited, roots sucking unselectively. And no running round, said Dr Shimshek, his kind eyes popping. I smiled. We skidded up to the Institute.

Fikri Dikmen lit the stove. I lay in bed. The vet and his cousin left me the paper. Dr Shimshek patted my blanketed foot. I watched their watery sunny heads float out of the gates. Now I was the hill of me. The chemicals fought there. What use was I? I couldn't even watch. So I went to sleep.

45   Shell Company

I woke up. Shell Company were standing round the bed with paper bags of chocolates tied up with ribbons. It could have been heaven. Get well soon, they said. I mightn't have anything. I had some chocolates. I felt slow. Waterbeads raced down the window. The gates gleamed. A dolmush slipped and slapped down Ali Emiri 4.

I sat up. The alien hole hurt me. My head was muggy with milk. The thought of sunshine frightened me.

Quick, said Fikri Dikmen. Let's go. He put me in a big grey coat. We had tea in the Institute tearoom. We drank in our coats. Come on, he said. Azize Ipek swayed in. She smiled with watery kindness. Here, she said, and gave me a grey umbrella. I smiled. Fikri Dikmen led me into Ali Emiri 4.

46   With an umbrella to no. 2

The city walls stood up deckled and black in the sky. Behind the grey clouds somewhere the sun beat on their tops. I looked up nervously round the umbrella. Fikri Dikmen splashed and splished ahead. Hurry, he said now and then. The statue of Atatürk looked especially grey in the cloudy morning light.

The sand buckets swarmed with raindrops. We hurried into the yellow room. Fikri Dikmen held the umbrella. It wet the floor like an incontinent bat. I watched the puddle smilingly. Fikri Dikmen took me out of the big grey coat. I got in the big leather couch. The nurse held up the little sharp alien and aimed it. In the left half of my stomach it ejaculated its helping of milk. Get well soon, said the nurse. She whispered to Fikri Dikmen. I shut my eyes and got back into the coat.

We splashed off. A white sheet like a leaf from a big white tree. The Council Bus Depot. Its tin rooves dripped. We hurried through the city walls. Fikri Dikmen stopped behind a bus. Have a cigarette, he said. My eyes rolled slowly. It can't hurt, he said. I

smiled. I nearly said. He hurried on, dragging a squiggle of smoke.
Thanks for all this.

Dr Shimshek rang. The Weekday Health Centre was between the
vegetable market and the football stadium. Quite close actually, he
said. Are you all right? I cried a bit.

47   Ramadan starts

Ramadan started. Hot blue and clear. Sunshine burned like a
blowtorch towards my bed. I leapt up. The hot square slithered
burning through the stove. I went red. And I still do go.

I bought a wet cheese from the shop across the other road. My
sickness as dispensation. I gobbled it. Red and wet, I hurried to the
Preparation Room. Azize Ipek swayed at her desk and wrote.
Good morning, she said waterily. I looked out the window at the
brown rosegarden. The blue sky burned like acid. How was I? I
smiled redly. A bit hot. She smiled. Oh, I'm hungry.

Fikri Dikmen threw the door open. Come on, he said. Quick. We
hurried out into Ali Emiri 4. The sun burned in my face. My ears
hurt. Atoms of alien milk unfolded like flowers just under my skin.
Their petalled dishes drank heat that burned it. In my cool
protected innards the rest hurried from place to place, looking for
suck.

Quick, said Fikri Dikmen, pulling a squiggle of smoke behind him
across the blue card of sky. We hurried past the football stadium.
Open Early and Late, said a restaurant. For Ramadan. Sunshine
flashed in the window. Someone was sellotaping newspaper to the
glass. That is to hide, said Fikri Dikmen, hypocrites. In the cool
protected innards flies hurried from place to place, looking for suck.

48   The Weekday Health Centre

We rattled down some concrete steps that crumbled under us. We
hurried into a dark waitingroom. The flowers closed. My skin

cooled. I smiled. We panted. Shapes crouched along the walls.
Come on, said Fikri Dikmen. He pulled my sleeve. The room
suddenly made itself long. A small window made it grey. And
yellow. Two concrete washingtubs hung off the wall. Taps dripped
red water into them clunkily. We squished onto spongy slatting.
The grey light lit up a big fridge in the corner. Cream chrome.
And yellow. Like a deSoto. Its engine idled. It wobbled and
buzzed. Something inside tinkled. Where's everyone? said Fikri
Dikmen to the window.

Alone on the yellowish half of a floating tabletop stood a new
sealed box of syringes. It gleamed dully. Made in Germany, it said.
I sat on a greenish bench. Into the new angle of yellow light leapt a
brown medical couch. It was held up by swoops of glinting steel
tubing. The suspension of a giant's pram. The couch coughed.
Lumps of horsehair leapt out through tears in the leather. I shut my
eyes.

Everyone wasn't there.

49   The little girl please

The fridge wobbled and buzzed. The box of syringes flickered
yellowishly. Morning! said a tall voice. We all turned round.

A nurse loomed out of the waitingroom. Her hair whirled up like
a chocolate-cream whirl. Morning, we said in the gloom. The little
girl please, she said. The nurse's pearl necklace popped like soap
bubbles. She cut the cellophane on the box with a fingernail.

An old man rattled in, stabbing the spongy slatting with two
walkingsticks. The nurse smiled. The little girl held the old man's
sleeve. The fridge idled and winked. The little girl's head was
wound round with bandages. The nurse picked up the little girl by
her neck and ankles and laid her in the couch. It stuck out some
hairy tongues. The little girl lay still. Seven dogs, said the nurse,
nodding at the ball of bandages. Can you imagine? His, she said,
nodding at grandad. She took a syringe, and a brown bottle out of
the fridge. I looked into the dark. In Tatvan, I heard her say. They

86

sleep here. Every night. Out there. Yellow light glinted along the questing needle.

50   The station was in the country

I climbed into the giant's pram. The next needle gleamed down through air and then flesh. I gasped. The nurse yanked it out, dripping milk. Get well soon, she said. Atoms of alien milk unfolded new buds just under my right skin. They spread. I went red. My ears burned. I gulped. Something wrong. Fikri Dikmen clack-clacked his beads. What are the shadows in the waitingroom? From some innard shackled to another. Fear. To all of them. I sat up.

The nurse was writing my Rabies Record Card. No. of Days. Ccs Administered. Keep it somewhere safe, she said smilingly. Her chocolate-cream hair whirled up. Course of Treatment. Name. I took it. Pink cardboard.

We hurried out. Sunshine slapped my face. I went redder. 2ccs. 14 days. 155.

We turned quickly into Ali Emiri 4. Fikri Dikmen said, when I was little the station was in the country. Ah, how fast Diyarbakir's grown. The city walls gleamed at the end of the road like a big hot black leather shoe.

51   Injection no. 4

I lay and watched the next needle pierce the air. My flesh didn't make any difference. In it went, sliding away. The nurse stopped. Oh, she said, wrong side. I dropped my pink record card. More fear. The selfish alien penis withdrew. It gleamed steelily.

My right side burned with blood. So near my skin it ached. Now and then it still does. I sleep on it. What a double! Half safe from everything. Half prey to anything. I sat up and leaned left. What use was that? I thought it would drain across, like snot in a nostril. I forgot my name. Get well soon, said the nurse.

I hurried away. The hot sun lit a carpet like a hanging garden from a high balcony. Three rights one left. I worried. Someone lay asleep across two chairs in front of a suit shop. A red egg stood under one chair. The too-used hole hurt. A hot bead sat in the hole in my skin. It let down a hot string through the empty road of the needle. I gasped.

I sat in the brown rosegarden. The sun went watery. I gulped water. Fear was elsewhere. The cure spread tendrils of panic out in my head. Which chemical was which? Did I suck fear not mine out of the hill? Did I make it and shake on a mountain of healthy earth and rocks? Did one disease them both?

Wait and see. Sweet rain fell. Sevtap pulled down the blind in the Institute tearoom. We had tea. The sugar glittered. My sickness was a dispensation. Sevtap had a cigarette. Her red lips smiled. So, she said guiltily, what?

Nejati Bey came in quietly. He drank his tea by the blind window. The vaccine is useless, he said. His amber beads clicked.

52   Injection no. 5

Next time the sun came up I felt cooler. I walked purposefully to the Health Centre. The little girl sat under a tree by the crumbly concrete steps. Grandad was asleep. His hat lay embroideredly in the grass. His head lay on her little knees. The sun slipped down his walkingstick. I smiled. The little girl's head, all wound round with bandages, looked away. I hurried down the steps.

The nurse unwrapped a new syringe. Left left left left, she said merrily. I climbed into the pram and bared my skin. The white cloud shaded in my blood. I thought, a better balance. Get well soon, she said.

Fikri Dikmen was waiting. Come on, he said. Quick. I got in. The red fish screeched off. The first bits of dust blown from the drying mud blew away dryly. A man ran past with twenty breadrings on his head. A folding chair snapped at his hand. We stopped at Fikri

Dikmen's house. We sat at the red formica table. Five done, said
Fikri Dikmen smiling. Have a cigarette. The white cloud spilled in
my skin, near the surface. The sun slapped my face. I went red.
We sat in the livingroom and watched TV. The screen looked
white. Some shadow moved. I clutched my left side. Stop stop. I
stood up. Fear. White cloud on the brain. I nearly said.

53   Monopoly in lentils

Come on, said Fikri Dikmen. Let's go out. We thuddered across
the Tigris. You can't beat these Murat stationwagons, he said. The
river looked yellow. We stopped by a big field of lentils. Come on,
said Fikri Dikmen. We stumbled into the lentils. Fikri Dikmen had
Monopoly under his arm. We sat in the lentils and played
Monopoly. I lost. The flickery sunlight burned my face now and
then like acid on a skinned rabbit. The lentils wobbled little threads
of shade here and there. What use was that? The Tigris moved on
and on and on. The big black walls of Diyarbakir loomed.

I shook emptily.

Fikri Dikmen put his arm round my neck. Don't worry, he said.
Let's have dinner. We had hamburgers. The sun went down in the
windows like running paint. I woke up. Fikri Dikmen's house was
dark. A red rug lay all over me. Folk songs shook the windows. I
got up and looked out.

Across the road in little playground floodlights a hundred school-
children were singing. A shining girl with a great pink bow on her
hair like a luminous night butterfly. Atatürk watched. A shining
boy in a shiny white collar bigger than his head. And a big sword
moon all yellow. Microphones like big night insects glinting in the
electric light, legs and necks. The headmaster conducted with a
gleaming walkingstick. His big shiny head blipped like a torch. I sat
down. I prickled all over. I cried just before I fell asleep. Can a tree
instruct a hill?

54   Some lonely tea

The Institute tearoom was full. Only my teaglass twinkled and
glittered. No smoke surged round the ceiling. In the still first flush
of faith and hope. The neon lights buzzed now and then. I felt
ashamed. God knows you're sick, said Nejati Bey decently. I smiled.

I hurried to my sixth injection. The sky ran with blue and clouds.
Like it was all tilted. I wondered what might slide off the horizon
next. Between clouds and clouds that slid down the blue slope. I
hurried more.

Two women with twisted legs sat on a green rug near the crumbly
concrete steps. A cloud slid along the top of the Health Centre. I
threw money at them. Another bit of faith and hope. Charity and
forgiveness. It's right, I thought. There's no proof. Why, I scrab-
bled down the steps, not?

55   Another rabid person

I blundered into the vaccination room. The spongy slatting
squished. The pram was full. The fridge wobbled and buzzed into
gear. Machineguns glinted in the grey light like big alien insects'
necks. A needle flashed like lightning. It slid into the pram. The
nurse was quiet. Shadows flibbled darkly behind the machineguns.
It slid out. Get up, barked a shadow. The barrels gleamed along
like carlights down a shiny grey road. My heart pushed and
battered blood and milk.

Out of the pram rose a big dark thing. Swoops of glinting steel
tubing bowed and squealed. It was a big prisoner. He stood like a
halfpainted tree in the yellowgrey light. The soldiers were suddenly
half alight: the nurse had opened the burbling fridge. The light cut
them out of the dark. They spat. The nurse unwrapped a new
syringe.

You got rabies? asked one of the soldiers decently. If I say no, then
strike me down. If I say yes, anyway I'll die. I smiled waterily. Get
well soon, said the two soldiers. The prisoner bowed. Handcuffs

snapped at his arms. They poked him out. When he reached the door the sunlight hugged him.

56   Injection no. 6

I climbed in. It was warm, and smelt of mud. I shut my eyes. He, said the nurse. I waited. I opened my eyes. She stood tally above the couch holding the syringe like a chef about to pipe icing onto a cake. A tiny glass blip of milk balanced on the end. Which would go in me. I stared. Her necklace popped like soap bubbles. Was bitten in prison, she said. As she swooped the needle down at my soft skin and innards it screamed. I sat up. Fear blushed me furiously. She stopped. The prison-jeep's siren faded. The nurse slid the needle deep into me. They're taking him back, she said. She was close. She pushed the piston. I smiled. Get well soon, she said closely. The long alien withdrew. The hill gathered back broken blood and bits in its wake. Why? It was made to. What could I do? Live or die.

Grandad was smoking under the wiry tree. The little girl's head wound round with bandages lay on his knees. The greening grass prickled at his shalvar. Clouds slid down the sky. Sunshine came next.

57   I forget

Now to tell the truth about nine o'clock. Azize Ipek curled her lips round a meatball. The lights in the Preparation Room zizzed. I went dizzy. Her greaseproof paper crackled. I stood up. I stared at the wall. People dancing on a lawn in Hakkari. With all the abandon of passing time. What use was that? I stared at the picture on the White Bank calendar. Find today for instance. I couldn't. What about the month? I've really no idea. Azize Ipek stirred her tea with a faraway tinkle. My brain went electric. In this evolutionary overdrive I melted. But the hill stayed. It was me, after all. But I didn't know anything about it. It was heavy. I thought I looked like a big hairy dungball plastered with dirt. Azize Ipek swayed at another meatball. I snatched at these inconsequentialities.

Safety. Terror didn't teach me much. Except what it felt like.
Roaring out of the earth. Which isn't much.

58   Flashing lights

The prison-jeep hurtled towards the Health Centre. I stepped
back. Leaves on the wiry tree signaled. Orange-black. Orange-
black. The sun burned in my face. My ears hurt. I burned into
overload. And meltdown. Atoms of alien milk hurled their petalled
dishes open just under my skin. They drank heat. They throbbed
with light. They shuttled with noise. I threw money at the two
women on the green rug. The wiry tree stuck out suddenly like
electrified hair. I staggered. I stumbled. Dribble swarmed over my
lip and fell like mercury into the greening grass. It moved there
like a glass worm.

The prison-jeep screeched stop by the crumbly concrete steps. I
put my hand on my heart. It wasn't there.

The big prisoner got out. Morning, he said. His handcuffs clanked.
They poked him down the crumbly steps.

I scampered in.

59   A queue for no. 7

There was a queue. We all held our pink Rabies Record Cards.
The little girl with her head wound round with bandages: grandad
on his sticks drilling into the squishy spongy slatting. The fridge
wobbled and buzzed. The nurse cut the cellophane on a new box
of syringes with her fingernail. Then the big prisoner, his head up
in the pink light: and the guards. Their halflit machineguns glinted.
The tap dripped red water. I was still well. The nurse laid the little
girl in the couch like a sultan turbaned into a pleasureboat. I
smiled. Something wound round my leg. The needle flashed. Next
into a grave to be shot. The nurse lifted the prisoner's rag. He
smelt of mud. My leg wobbled. The pink light licked the needle as
it fell. I turned round.

92

A little boy was holding my leg. Because then he could hold one foot off the floor. It was tied up in a sheet. Petals of blood panted through the white. He smiled. His shaved head gleamed fuzzily.

The nurse swept him up into her arms. His face stayed the same. She pushed the needle in. His little stomach fluttered like a bit of hardboard.

When the milken army ran to its places between each sentry already there and made a white plain just under my skin I bowed in my mind to my friends. Would it march in or out? I climbed out of the pram.

60   Smoking

The sky curled blue with a soft wind. The soldiers passed their cigarette between them. Their machineguns stood against the wiry tree. The greening grass rattled. The little boy smoked like the punctuation in a fast sentence. His smoke danced. So, I thought, what? God knows we're all ill. Or weak. Like everyone.

61   Four short visits

In the afternoon Nezahat Ipliji took me to the post office. She worked on floor four and a half. She showed me the phone wires. The wooden room was high and sunlit. I smiled. We had tea. It might have been five minutes. The boysoldiers on guard at the door stared at the sun.

Erkan Yazirchioglu took me to a pancake restaurant in Office. The air was cold inside. The windows were covered with newspapers. Open Early and Late. For Ramadan. He sat in pleasing abstinence and I ate. Some men in dim cold corners hurried food down themselves. Their reputations protected by a business they had been kind enough to patronise at the peril of their souls. Erkan plopped sugar in my tea. It swirled and glittered dully. You're sick, he said. Drink up.

We hurried to a green cardhouse. No smoke surged round the ceiling. Then to a greener billiardroom. I drank tea everywhere. Erkan smiled. When I got home I ran the tap. I said my name and address. I dreamed that the dancers on the White Bank calendar all had one foot wound up in a sheet. Petals of blood panted through the white. Flowers danced in the greening grass.

62   Children's Bayram

I woke up, got up, and adjusted my thick head. My armpit hurt. I drank Lezzo. The pain went away. An April shower fell on my window. The waterbeads raced down. The sun shone now and then. The clouds passed here and there.

I looked down at my stomachskin. Four rights, three lefts. Blotches pushed and itched there like small bloody heads trying to get out. I cried. The clouds raced away. The sun hit the waterbeads. My room filled with light. It slipped and slid round the walls. The uneven armies of milk opened their dishes. My right side prickled and burned. I should be balanced. The left blotches prickled and burned. I blushed. Right today. Five–three. Why? The worst day.

It was Children's Bayram. I hurtled out the gates. I raced through the city walls. They were black and heavily warmed. Salt burned in a nutcart. A tank burbled under some lime trees, flickered with bits of blue shade. I slapped on towards the hospital. Bang bang. Round the corner came the Diyarbakir Children's Massed Band. They headed for Atatürk. I leaped back against the recordshop window. My back went cold. Their bugles flashed goldly. I was late. The drums banged with my heart. They burned past, all red and gold. I galloped off.

The nurse had come especially on Saturday and a holiday. Oh it's nothing, she said. She closed the door. The big red leather couch aahed like a mouth. I got in. Right right right, she said merrily. I smiled and shut my eyes.

I pulled up my shirt. Oh dear, she said. Fear yanked my innards. The light yellowy air moved. I opened one eye. The buttery walls

glistened. Boff boff. The Children's Band. The bugles parped. The
nurse marched back to the couch, smiling kindly. Cotton bud, she
said, waving one hand. Alcohol, she said, waving the other. Bing
bang. I closed my eyes.

63   No. 8 in the right side

She dabbed my blotches. I got an erection. The yellow light lapped
at my eyelids. Clish clash. The Children's Band. My stomach
fluttered gaspingly. The bodies of the blotches smiled coolly deep
in my innards. I opened my eyes. She dabbed a bit more. I closed
my eyes. I gasped like I was walking into a cold sea. The needle
slid its silvery length through my skin. It spiked slowly on and on.
It pierced heavy red curtains that stretched against the point and
then slid back along the spike. It stopped. I breathed shallowly.
Leave it in. My back arched a bit. I groaned. Then like white
cream ejaculated into a bowl of cherries the milky serum spread
out creamily. It curled off. The needle stayed, deliciously. Crash
bang. The Band marched at the hospital. I squirmed against the
metal bodkin. The last creamy blob gushed out. It still stayed. I
gasped. It slid out slowly like immortality withdrawing from
corruption. Aaah, I said.

I glowed through the anteroom. The big prisoner was standing
under the pick and shovel crossed. Morning, he said. Morning, I
said smilingly. The guards poked him in. The Massed Children's
Band was playing the national anthem at the glass doors of the
hospital. Patients and nurses leaned out of the windows like doves
in a great big dovecote, and sang. The children sparkled like hope.

64   A snooze in the park

I wandered towards home. Republic Park was full. Balloons like
bits of sensible freedom bobbed here and there. A few clouds
wound along the blue sky jerkily. Breadringsellers splodged the air
with bready smells. I sat on the greening grass. It prickled my
trousers. Little girls in party dresses frothed round the bushes.
Orange and purple and lace. I smiled. A little girl sailed past and

touched her big white cowboy hat at me like a gentleman. I was still well. I sparkled dully like hope discovered again. Not lost but mislaid.

I got up purposefully. There was nothing to be done except get on. As if that is not enough. Life's decorations frothed and swirled round me. I thought I was strong. My leaves glittered with sunlight and I forgot the heavy determinism of my roots. What use was that? Spring threw me up. I picked a leaf. I marched along the grass. A photographer went snap. Where's the kids? he said. I smiled. Suddenly tired, I sat down in the grass again. My blotches itched. The sun rolled down. I puffed. Nutsellers. Sweetsellers. Icecream.

I snoozed.

65   Nejati Bey

I woke up, got up, and looked around. The sun and its creatures were gone. A soldier in a white helmet and white puttees clattered away down a path. The big high swooping vague blue monument in the middle of the park swooped up vaguely. I hurried home.

Nejati Bey tapped on my window. We hurried through the city walls. A new hoarding picked round with lightbulbs was nailed up on the gate. The People Are The Thing, it read brightly. So they are. We went to an expensive pastryshop. There were no newspapers on the windows. I ate baklava and drank Pepsi while Nejati Bey clicked his amber beads sourly. He looked at me pityingly. I smiled. All round children ate glittery sugary things. Two waiters with long yellow horseheads and bushes of black hair swished among the tables. They are famous, said Nejati Bey gloomily, freaks.

66   Get well soon you all

Birds trilled frantically through the trelliswork. The brown rosegarden distilled its rosy smell in the hot earth. My window sparkled. I hurried out. The sun hugged me warmly. My head buzzed. I was still well.

The sun let rip. I gasped. I reached the six bloody buckets. I rushed under the pick and shovel crossed. I marched into the little ante-room. My pink Rabies Record Card fluttered. Men in flatcaps sat on benches all round the place. God be with you. The nurse threw open the door. Yellow light leapt out and hurled itself all over them. Their moustaches bristled and sparkled. Their wet old eyes glimmered. Old men's tetanus day, whispered the nurse as I hurried past. The plastic pearls round her neck melted meltingly.

I pulled up the left side of my shirt. I smiled and shut my eyes. The yellow light swam round my eyelids. She dabbed my blotches with cotton bud and alcohol. A sweet coolness like a little rainshower grew in a cloud off my skin. It fell on the little landscape of my stomach breathingly. I squirmed happily. I opened my eyes. The nurse waved the new syringe in a sea of light. Her hair whirled. The flibbleflabble lapping lit the milk inside. I wanted to drink it. Left left left, she said merrily.

The time it happened like a simile.

I hurried out into the anteroom. Get well soon! all the old men yelled. I smiled widely. And get well soon you all, I yelled back. We all bowed completely. I burst out into the sunshine transfixed, itching and beaming.

67   No snoozing in the park

I jaunted towards home. Republic Park was empty. I sat down. The grass prickled my trousers. Fear gasped out of my chest. It shot up my neck. It brayed like a bugle in my brain. A lightbugle. I had no idea. I stayed wide awake. The big high swooping blue vague monument in the middle of the park made me gasp. The sun hit me. I blushed. Atoms of milk ran round and changed places just under my skin. Like musical chairs. I heated up until bing like an oven I reached my highest heat. I shook there hotly. What? I didn't explode. I was still well.

I hurried home. I bought some Ramadan bread. It was plaited on top. And sesameseeded. I ran the tap. Ah. I splashed water round the bathroom walls. I flooded the floor. I sat under the shower. I laughed haha. It might be brain damage. Well at least the horror would be only darkly understood. The bread got soggy. I dried my clothes from a wire by the stove. I had taken off a skin. I felt cold.

That night Nejati Bey brought me a puzzle-ring in a black box. He clacked his amber beads and looked at me pityingly. Like I'd never work it out before I. We hurried to the Labour Cinema. Nejati Bey snorted gloomily at the film. He leaned over. The sound is not, he whispered sadly, synchronised. Behind us somebody nibbled seeds with the fury of a suit full of fieldmice. The floor was a drift of husks that whispered when I sighed.

I stumbled home itching and frowning. Only my ears burned. I could have sat in a desert and cooled off.

68   Set free by sheep

I woke up and got up slowly. My window was a blue square written on by the Institute gate. Nothing moved. I heard the salepman yelling. His tincart rattled the air. But nothing moved. Fear whooshed up in me. My heart banged. It was still only me. I waited for a bird. The sky stayed still. The gates were wrought. But didn't wright. I hurried round and round the room. It was still only me. The world stuck outside like a giant cube of gelatin. I went mental.

My clothes hung on the wire by the stove. I thought they were me. So what was I then? I didn't dare open the door. A clearplastic stone sat outside. As big as everything. What was the most frightening thing? That I couldn't say it was like anything. Something like that. It wasn't like anything I could think of. How could my little fury loosen such a huge coagulation? It pressed the glass. I gasped. Hard to breathe. I smelt salep. But nothing moved. It wasn't like anything. I crouched against the wall. Sunlight speared the gelatin world like a yellow plastic ruler. I cried. The sun got hotter. But nothing moved. I closed my eyes. I put my arms over my head. I bobbed on my hams.

Clish.

I looked out. Azize Ipek swam through the wrought gates. Bits of the world like bubbles or broken bits of glass soared crackling off her shoulders. She unfurled across the path. Her black hair made slow currents here and there. So the world unfixed. It was still slow. The gate hung open, written sideways on the blue sky. A flock of sheep pattered through solemnly. They bobbed on towards my window. Bits of the world scampered like hopping fleas off their backs. They stopped at the glass. They looked in. A bird rattled through the evaporating sky. Their eyes, green and solemn, stared at me. I stood up.

The shepherd stood at the gate. He yelled. The sheep stared at me, greeneyed and solemn. I swam about in my yellowish aquarium stupidly. They looked in and looked at each other. The shepherd waved his walkingstick. His shalvar flapped. The sheep still stared. The shepherd flapped amongst them. Bits of the world fizzed off his big knitted hat like fireworks. He looked in. I bowed. He hurried off, slapping his sheep. They bobbled out of the gates and back into Ali Emiri 4.

The smell of salep and droppings danced round in the sunbeams. Bikecarts and little vans rushed up and down Ali Emiri 4. Birds swooped here and there. Bits fell off the block of flats being built next door. The postman wheeled his bike through the Institute gates.

I got dressed.

69   Rubbish

I hurried to the Weekday Health Centre. My card flapped. I threw money at the two women on the green rug. Ominously, I had plenty of time to watch the coins make their ways tumblingly through the blue air. I walked faster. Though one leg was a bit glassy and the other a bit gluey. I wasn't deranged. I don't think. Charity and something. Deserts. I stopped.

A wall on the front of the Health Centre had fallen down entirely. Or it was me? I hopped and danced on the prickling lime grass to keep at bay the climbing horrors that come from silence and stillness. What use was that? A big yellow crane like an alien creaked noddingly on the first floor. Its metal neck stuck up through the roof. I was seeing things. But they were there. I mean generally. I gasped.

Help came. Climbing sirens brought the big prisoner nearer and nearer. The little girl with her head wound round with bandages glided out from the wiry tree. The little boy with his foot done up in a sheet carried his shaved head carefully forwards like a melon on a plate. He put his little arms round my leg. I cried. So much I forgot to ask, was there a crane?

We hurried to the crumbly concrete steps. Piles of charred paper flapped like piles of pressed birds. We tiptoed through the pricking grass. One little long cloud like a line of chalk floated in the sky. Oildrums lay on their sides bleeding oil. I looked up distrustfully. The yellow alien nodded. We rushed on. It took ages. Puddles of rotted fruit and vegetables bobbed, yawned and sweated in the limegreen grass. Speared. We tiptoed round and round. Then suddenly we slipped down the crumbly concrete steps together and disappeared.

70   Injection no. 10

We lay under the nurse one after the other like hems under a sewingmachine. Right right right, she said merrily. It wasn't that I didn't feel anything. But I didn't have any something. Reverberations. Get well soon, she said. I smiled. I worried. I might be desensitised. Brainhard. Unable to see the horror this time. I worried not that the horror had gone, but that I had lost the sensitivity to see it. I gasped. I hurried out. The sun hit me in the face. I went red. I was still well. The new horror at not finding horror filled me like an injection. Atoms of alien milk unfolded new buds just under all my skin and beat. My ears burned. I gulped. Good. Familiar fear. Usual fire. I galloped off towards Ali Emiri 4. The crane nodded in the breeze. Its yellow metal neck creaked above the roof.

71   Spies

The Director of the Institute was waiting at the twisted gates. His suit shone if black can. The long thin cloud glided over the sky. He grabbed my arm. He pushed me solicitously behind a small pillar. His neat moustache sat like a scrubbingbrush on the table of his lip. It waggled. His beautiful round black eyes rolled conspiratorially. Emergency, he whispered. The Institute's Turkish flag dropped all the way down from its pole to the neat short thick black hair on the Director's head. There are spies, he said. The sun beamed. The flag shifted suspiciously a bit nearer. Around about, he said. My blotched right side prickled and itched. Be careful, he said. I was surprised. His neat moustache waggled. I smiled. I worried. Be careful.

He hurried out the gates. His shiny black shoes clicked and clacked. He waved at a taxi. They disappeared in a swarm of dust. I shook a bit. I sweated. I hurried inside. The flag stroked the blue air. The clouds poled on.

72   Nice plaited bread

I bought something to eat at the shop across Ali Emiri 4. The bread was soft and white and woven in beautiful plaits. I ate it in the brown rosegarden. Ali the caretaker arrived with a hose. Morning, he said. I smiled. The sky gleamed bluely. A voice went past the gates yelling lemons lemons. I closed my eyes. I heard Ali turn on the tap. The water fell. Perhaps he'd gone mad. The Director I mean. The sun warmed my ears, which didn't go red. I chewed a piece of nice plaited bread. He was seeing things maybe. Swishswosh. I nearly dropped off. The sun beamed. I opened my eyes. An arch of waterdrops glittered through the blueness fallingly. What use was that? How lovely. The roses jiggled under a tapping rain. The soil pittered and puffed. The sun sparkled. Ah. I chewed another piece of nice plaited bread. I stood up. There was plenty to worry about. So I started again.

73   A sweaty night

I woke up, got up, and ran to the taps. I was still well. Sweat dribbled in the hot hollow on the top of my breastbone. The water swarmed down the plughole. Waterdrops raced round the sink. Bits and pieces flew off. They spattered the walls. The moon looked in lemonly. It slowly rose through my window. The twisted gates gleamed. Spray slapped my face and chest with little fingers. Pitterpatter. I drank under the tap. Water dribbled down my legs. I dreamed that a bus called Siverek drove a syringe into my head. I tripped over my shoes. I fell down and snapped my toothbrush. I cried. I woke up. I'd already got up. My back dribbled with sweat. I put the sheet between my teeth. I was still well.

The heat came like I was blottingpaper put in a plate of hot red ink. It flew up me, seeping hungrily. I gasped. I jumped out of bed. It pushed beads of sweat out of me as it rose. I dripped. My skin burned. Tiny hot drops stuck on the end of each hair. I stood still like a hot glass statue. The mountain got ready the tree to die by shooting its roots full of anaesthetic. I swayed. I toppled. I woke up.

Two wire worms of blood slid slowly out of my old dogholes. Like red railwaylines they lengthened parallelly. I stood by the window and watched them slide out of my body. They curved upwards, gleaming slightly. I gagged like a cat having grass pulled out of its throat. The red worms slowly pulled themselves out across the room and started to glide together over the bed. I grabbed the windowsill. The moon spied on me with lemony interest. I was sick on the floor. The red worms undulated slightly as they nosed over the sink together. Sweat rolled down my legs. Their blunt blind red noses reached the door. They waved about round the doorknob a bit like baffled snakes. I thought they mustn't get out. I couldn't touch them. Wind them in. Or cut them off. I didn't know the somethings. Consequences. The moon rose disdainfully behind the glass. I roared. The moon went on. The night had hours of darkness left. They tangled the doorknob messily. They slipped instead of turning it. Sweat hung on my skin. My eyes stung. The doorknob glinted. It turned a little bit. I held my breath. My body was emptying. More slid out, slackening the ropes between me and the door. I was seized with a fear so great I started to talk. Gurgled whispering.

They heard me. They slowly, inquisitively lifted their heads from the wet doorknob and turned slowly to look at me with blunt blind red noses. I said goodbye to the part of me I knew. They reared. My surroundings shut up shop. I stood on a pinhead. They made mouths. And teeth. They dribbled and snapped. The moon excused itself. They reared higher.

Then they shot at me. They arrived before I yelled. They parted in front of my nose like a jet display team. Each took one ear. In their horrible hot little red teeth. And lifted me off the floor. Slowly we drifted across the room. Their ropes thrashed and tangled. Sweat pitterpattered off me all the way down to the sheet. Splat. Splot. Could I keep them out? We glided above the bed. The tap and the sink flicked little waterdrops at us. They hissed and turned to steam like bubbles on a hotplate. We reached the wall. My ears stretched. I covered my penis with my hands. They pressed me to the wall. I panted and gasped. The remains of moonlight painted my destruction light lemon and dust. This arrangement lasted a minute or two. Charity and hope. Brainhard. Dogdead.

I hung there for ages. I swung slightly in the failing moonlight. I think I fell asleep in despair. Hanging in the air and flattened sometimes against the wall. Held there by monsters of my own sickness. When I woke up in a raincoat of sweat the tap was still running. Cold waterbeads flicked all round me. The wall was wet. The top of the stove dripped. The moon had rolled round the sun for me. It peeped in the window at horror, but missed what had made it. I had the form of it still. The rest tangled, fading in the invisible air, round my body, which was lying on the floor. A bit yellowy. One hand had nearly got to the sheet. I felt the gluey sweatballoons blobbing out all over me, like bubblegum blown out from a million little hot mouths. Well, it was a hot morning. The glass was slashed with sunshine.

74 A new purpose

I thought the hill would go on anyway. Doing what it did. Or
what it must. Darkly. So my state of mind was to put it bluntly
irrelevant. I thought I might as well be cheerful.

After that.

The sky was bright clear blue and hot. I got dressed purposefully.
The sun beamed. I smiled back. I hurried to the Institute tearoom
and had tea. The sugar swished beautifully. The sun danced on the
formica tabletops. Sevtap clickclacked down the corridor with
letters. Azize Ipek floated about nervously. The Director was in. I
purposefully entered the Preparation Room. Azize Ipek was
writing. I said good morning. Fikri Dikmen lay in his chair and
stared sideways out the window at the less brown and greening
rosegarden. Good morning, they said. I sat down. He's back, said
Fikri Dikmen, clacking his beads. Azize Ipek smiled waterily. I
know, I said. I didn't mention spies. I looked at Fikri Dikmen. The
roses waved their green shoots at the sun. I nearly said. He sat up.
He had a very bad time, said Azize Ipek. Tears lay in her eyes
gleamingly. Apparently, she added, swaying back to her writing.
Haha, said Fikri Dikmen, looking sideways out the window.

This arrangement lasted for a bit. Which worried me. I got up
purposefully. Come on, I said to Fikri Dikmen. I tapped my
watch. Let's go. He leapt out of his chair. We raced down the
corridor and through the twisted gates. The city walls gleamed like
liquorice. Dust danced in the yellowy air. We hurried off to the
Health Centre.

75 Rewards of having a new purpose

The sun beat down goldenly. We rushed past the Atatürk Football
Stadium. Stop, said Fikri Dikmen. We stopped in a cloud of
sunfilled dust. Look, he said. Diyarbakirspor vs Erzurumspor. He
tapped the paper poster with a hot finger. Tomorrow, he said. I
smiled. Good, I said. I meant that will suit my new purpose. We
rushed on.

The fallen down entirely wall throbbed in the heat. Quick, said Fikri Dikmen. I had slowed down to find some money for the women on the green rug. Charity and forgiveness. Health and Something. Strength. The big yellow crane creaked noddingly on the first floor. No similes. We hurried through the prickling grass. No somethings. The wiry tree stuck up twistedly. Reverberations. In the hot blue sky. The little girl with her head wound round with bandages was asleep in the black black muslin shade with grandad. His little hat had rolled onto the grass. His head bowed into her arm. Oildrums lay on their sides bleeding oil. The prisoner was late.

Puddles of rotted fruit and vegetables steamed round our feet. The little boy stood at the top of the crumbly concrete steps. We hurried down together into the only halfdark waitingroom. My skin cooled. Nothing else happened. Fikri Dikmen stumbled in the halfdark. I nearly said again.

The small window was bright yellow and threw a girder of bright sunlight through the room. A figure of speech. It made itself long. The tap dripped orange water brightly. The fridge wobbled and buzzed. The nurse slit open the cellophane on a new box of syringes with her fingernail.

76   How painless no. 11 was

How painless it was. The needle slid in purposefully, ejaculated and withdrew. A way of saying it more true than not. The serum was carried off to needy places. I smiled. Fikri Dikmen clacked his beads. The siren approached.

The prisoner had a bandage round his head. His skin was yellow. His face was grizzled. The guards poked him in. Like a. No. I hurried past. Morning, I said quickly. He didn't answer. I stopped. He stood still like. No. Quick, said Fikri Dikmen. Let's go. We stumbled up the stairs. The sun slapped me in the face. My heart battered with confusion. I dropped my pink card. 2ccs. I was still falling. I gasped.

Alien petals unfolded slowly just under all my skin. I burned. I cried. Help, I said. From these figures of speech. Fikri Dikmen rushed on ahead.

77   Two useful presents

The Director had left a present on my desk wrapped in pink paper. Worrybeads made of scented plumstones. With a yellow tassel. Erkan Yazirchioglu had left me a bottle of Caladryl for my itch. Aren't people kind, said Azize Ipek waterily, swaying at the window, waiting for dark.

78   A bit of good advice but a bit late

If you get attacked by a dog, said Ahmet in the Institute tearoom. He stopped and glugged his tea. Its amber meniscus sparkled with sugar. Crouch down, said Suleyman into the space. He stirred his tea tinklingly. Ahmet nodded right. And it'll go away, finished Ahmet, while Suleyman gulped his golden tea. The glass flashed. I smiled. Thanks, I said. You're welcome, said Suleyman.

Darkness got dark enough. Azize Ipek opened her plastic lunchbox. She looked in and lifted out a meatball. Ahmet hurried away. Suleyman smiled sheepishly. Bon appetit, we said. She waved meatball number two and said, it's really hard to put more than two adjectives in the right order in a different language. I nodded happily.

I hurried across the sweetscented rosegarden to my door. The moon hung like a slice of lemon above the halfbuilt block of flats next door. Wooden scaffolding poles stuck through it like cocktail sticks. A bit fell off. The block of flats. And crashed down on the Institute fence. I marched purposefully at my door. Suddenly something leapt out from the unmoonlit wall and barked at me madly. I gasped. I staggered back. Mad dog, mad dog, squealed Fatih Öztürk. He hiccupped with laughter. Then he rushed out through the twisted gates into Ali Emiri 4, which ran past the Institute like a yellow river, moonlit and rippled with long long

shadows. I smiled at some stars that had just pricked through the
black hemisphere of night and permission. I stamped inside.

79 Adventure with a waterjug

As I hurried to my twelfth injection, I started to worry. There's no
point, but it can't be helped. Illogical, involuntary, ineffectual. I
stopped at the end of Ali Emiri 4. The sun fell on the city walls
like a lion on a panther. Sweat popped out of my forehead. Like a
tree waving its leaves around I flapped my worry here and there in
the hot sun. But it came from. Somewhere else. That hill. The
smallest bit of me I knew watched while the rest did a sort of
automatic semaphore. I sweated some more. Not with heat, I
thought. My heart fluttered like a bit of hardboard. I waved my
arms. I worried myself. I walked in all directions. I gasped. I verti-
goed. I thought the tide of milky serum was swooshing on and on
like waves against the tide of rabid germs. I sat on the grass near the
chemist's. I wiped my face with my sleeve. I thought it had got to
depend on its daily reinforcements. I thought it didn't make a
chemical change. Aah. So I worried about the end of my treat-
ment. I thought it would be followed by the victory of darkness,
madness, froth etcetera. I huddled up in a little hot ball on the
grass. My shirt got dusty. I thought why would the bit of me that
made me think make me think that?

An old woman with a big tin waterjug stopped and looked at me. I
unrolled. Have a breadring, she said. I took one out of her barky
hand. She crouched beside me and ate one of her own. I thought
the answer was. The old woman munched with her head on one
side to engage her back teeth. Her old toes gripped inside her
plastic sandals. Her pink headscarf pinged sequins in the hot sun.
She poured some water into her mouth from the jugspout. Have
some water, she said.

I opened my mouth. She poured the water in. I forgot the answer.
Like two figures on a figured fountain we crouched there transfer-
ring water. This arrangement lasted a moment or two. Water
dribbled down my neck. The sun threw heat all over the place
witheringly. The old woman stood up. Get well soon, she said. Ah

the old, the ill. I smiled. I was still well. Her sandals puffed away in the dust like birds walking over a cloud.

80   Twelve right

I was late. I made up my own mind. Be blank, I thought. See what happens then, you dark evolutionary things. I climbed into the couch blankly. Right right right, said the nurse merrily. I shut my eyes. Except they were me too. The things. I heard the nurse slit open a new box of syringes with her fingernail. I lay blankly in the pram. The needle punctured me against the resistance of my skin. I knew because the swoops of glinting steel tubing creaked down in a kind of squealing compression like a pram's suspension. Then pushed me back up round the needle with a squeaky decompression. I lay pierced blankly. She pressed the plunger. Something filled me up shallowly. From a hole. I felt the milky ejaculation spread just under the skin on my stomach. I wanted to die. To be blank is dead. To be an evolutionary object is dead. To look too far and deep is miserable, unfathomable, vertiginous. Evolution has given us a bit of playful decoration to pass the time pleasantly with while it gets on. Let's do that.

81   That's the new new purpose

That's the new new purpose.

82   Freed from the disease if not the treatment

Get well soon, said the nurse. I was still well. I rushed home. Perhaps they were all better too. That's it. The girl with her head wound round with bandages. The prisoner who smelt of mud. The little boy with his foot bound up in a sheet from Siirt.

The road along the Atatürk Stadium was full of playful decorative sorts of things. Good. I marched purposefully into them. Breadringsellers, lemoncarts, nutmen, used iron, horses, men in blue turbans. The sun yelled down. I whooped. All my life left now to be shallow. I lit up like a tilley lamp. I hissed. I radiated. I glowed.

I raced down Ali Emiri 4. Fikri Dikmen was standing at the gates of the Institute in a fizzing white shirt. When he saw me he jumped up and down. I stopped. He waved more. He jumped up and down. I raced at him puzzledly. Hooray hooray, he yelled, going up and down. What what? I said. He whirled his worrybeads like a lasso. To catch happiness. The vet's rung the vet's rung. He grabbed me round my neck. His shirt fizzed whitely. I shut my eyes. Then I opened them. The twisted gates whirled over my head, piercing the sun over and over like arrows into a golden bullseye. The dogs of Ergani, he yelled, bouncing up and down with me, are com-plee-tlee-hell-thee!

I fell on the street. My elbow bled. I cried. Fikri Dikmen danced round me clacking and whirling his beads. Com-per-leeeet-lee-hell-theeee, he yelled. I could have gambled and done nothing. Darkness madness and froth evaporated like spit on a hotplate. I was still well. I thought the serum. Death by side effects. I stood up purposefully. My head swayed. The sun banged congratulations on it. Fikri Dikmen smiled like a new piece of paper in the sun. I grabbed him. I thought not the serum. Thanks, I said. Oh have a cigarette, he yelled. Who cares? Let's have tea. We're going to the football. Hooray.

83 Tea

An army major was drinking tea in the Institute tearoom. We clinked our glasses. The neon light duelled with the sunbeams. The sugar swirled and sparkled. The sun slashed a yellow sword of light over his uniform. Bon appetit, he said fatly. Whatever you like. As long as it's not.

84 Diyarbakirspor vs Erzurumspor part 1

We raced purposefully to the stadium. People dressed as water-melons raced purposefully in the same direction. We raced through the narrow gates in a stew of red and green fruit and bunting. A man with a drum boomed in sideways. The sun let itself down a bit and burned right over the stadium. Fikri Dikmen fizzed. We burst into the stadium.

I stared at the earth arena. A conflict outside me. Good. I thought, can I be in something furious, free as I am now of the something furious that was in me? Watermelons bounced round me shouting. Dust swirled dustily.

Fikri Dikmen pulled my shirt. Here, here, he yelled. We sat down suddenly on the concrete terrace. It was hot. Fikri Dikmen yanked out two cigarettes recklessly. This is brilliant! he said, squiggling smoke at the sun. Watermelons smoked round us. His beads went clikettyclickettyclackettyclack at double speed. I grinned.

Suddenly a fire engine shot out of the players' tunnel and burst onto the pitch. The watermelons stood up and howled. Its bells clanged. It hurtled round the pitch in figuresofeight. The dust swirled and danced. Fikri Dikmen snorted happily. Men in flapping shalvars hung onto the fire engine. They jumped wildly and furiously up and down the handles and footles of the hurtling machine. The watermelons danced. Then the hose came on. The crowd screamed with delight. The men in flapping shalvars fell off the back and got watered. Fikri Dikmen started to choke. I jumped up and down. This is brilliant! said Fikri Dikmen.

The crowd honked with excitement. The row in front of us put their arms round each other's shoulders and danced in a big long line. Fikri Dikmen swayed. My ears went red. The fire engine swayed and slewed under the sun. Someone behind us collapsed with laughter haha. Then the fire engine shot back down the tunnel. Then the wet men. Fikri Dikmen coughed. Tears spilled out of his eyes. Oh oh, he said. We gasped. Dust floated into our mouths. The sun sparkled it.

85   Diyarbakirspor vs Erzurumspor part 2

I caught my breath somewhere. Suddenly hundreds of policemen

110

of a kind I hadn't seen before marched out of the tunnel. The ground went bomp bomp bomp bomp. They wore bottlegreen helmets. The watermelons booed and spat. The police waved their shields, truncheons and pistols. The little bald redandgreen hugely moustached man beside me shouted bastards bastards and threw his packet of plain biscuits at them. Then he jumped up and down on a carton of cherryjuice until it bled.

The teams ran on. Rolls of toiletpaper unwound in the blue sky and fluttered down over the stadium. Green and red bunting shot out of the terraces like flak from a trench. Watermelons and men in shalvars danced greenly and redly along the concrete. We bounced. We tangled ourselves in red and green and toiletpaper fluttered down and joined us all together whitely. This is brilliant! said Fikri Dikmen. We were beside ourselves with happiness.

Across the pitch, under the scoreboard sponsored by the White Bank, the desperately faithful fans, holding above them a long long banner that said Born for Diyarbakirspor, Die for Diyarbakirspor, hurtled, demented, in all directions, banging their drums, blowing their zornas, and pogoing from side to side in an ecstasy brought on with more delicious madness by shaking their heads like balloons on sticks.

Erzurumspor scored first. There was a terrible silence in the Atatürk Stadium. The sun spun quietly. The clouds paused. Fikri Dikmen went whiter. The watermelons sagged. The linesman who had not flagged the bastard scorer offside rushed from the pitch and down the tunnel on little wings of dust. He was replaced by a man in a luminous yellow shellsuit.

A minute before halftime, Diyarbakirspor struck back. Mehmet Itch let fly a shot so furious it knocked the Erzurum goalkeeper flat into the ground. The watermelons battered and boffed together in slow motion with anticipatory kisses and howls. The goalkeeper lay completely still, while the ball left him at great speed and smacked into the post. We gasped. Our heads moved together. Right. The ball was pushed slowly flat against the post, then it decompressed and shot into the back of the net. Left.

The stadium erupted. Drums and zornas thumped and squealed. The sky was splashed red and green like a gigantic automatic painting. The row in front of us did a selection of southeastern folkdances. Confetti, blown out of cardboard tubes, whirled into the air. The sun was silently taken aback, and retreated above the stadium. The confetti twinkled down onto the hot concrete terraces, our hair, shoulders and down our shoes. The goal, to the furious delight of everyone who was still conscious, then folded neatly sideways and collapsed onto the Erzurum goalkeeper, who was left like a fish in a net in a sea of dust.

The teams trotted away down the tunnel.

Halftime.

86   Diyarbakirspor vs Erzurumspor part 3

An ambulance hurtled out onto the pitch. The goalkeeper lay still, netted and dusted. The ambulance drove round and round the edge of the pitch, trailing bunting, flags and toiletpaper and swirled about with confetti, blowing its horn and its siren. The fanatics under the White Bank scoreboard hooted and jeered. The ambulance turned on all its lights, skidded across the centre circle, and disappeared down the tunnel.

We waited, agog.

The Erzurum trainer sprinted on. He rushed at the goalkeeper. Bastard bastard, yelled the little bald redandgreen hugely moustached man beside me. The trainer pulled the goalkeeper free by his armpits. The dust swarmed. Oh have a cigarette, said Fikri Dikmen. I took it without looking. A fat man with a hammer and two boys dressed as small watermelons pulled the goal back up, banged it and bowed.

The teams trotted out.

Mehmet Itch waved and bowed in all directions. The watermelons waved back. The whistle blew. The Erzurum team attacked him furiously. He disappeared redly and greenly. The fanatics under the White Bank scoreboard clawed at their fence. Some swarmed over. They thundered dustily towards the fight. The Diyarbakirspor trainer ran on with his medicine bag. They all met boff in the middle. Dust shot up in plumes and twists. A photographer so fat he had to walk sideways under a white panamahat edged into the dust and raised his camera.

The bottlegreen police charged. The sun withdrew further, a bit nervously.

In half an hour the game restarted. The bottlegreen police stood round the pitch. Fikri Dikmen clattered his beads furiously. The watermelons waited fatly in red and green suspense. The score- board side was seething like a surfeit of salmon trying to jump up a waterfall. Mehmet Itch sat on the sideline, unhurt. The referee blew the whistle.

Then Diyarbakir scored.

Pistachio husks and sunflower seeds darkened the sun. Which rolled behind a long thin cloud. The drums thumped like rejoicing hearts. Fikri Dikmen said, Oh! Brilliant! We grabbed each other and jumped up and down. The watermelons went ballistic, pinging off each other like billiardballs.

And in the last minute the Erzurum no. 9 kicked the ball out of the Diyarbakir goalkeeper's hands, from where it ran out behind the goalline, recollected it with his feet and, pretending that he was about to score, scored.

The world waited.

The referee yelled, disallowed! and disappeared down the players' tunnel, followed by the remaining linesman.

A riot ensued.

The man in the luminous yellow shellsuit did not make the tunnel.
He was punched in the mouth by a man in a white suit. I watched
in slow motion. The police advanced and battered people furiously
with their truncheons. The little bald redandgreen hugely mous-
tached man beside me hurled his shoes into the dusty arena. A
party of sweating men in dark suits stood in the VIP box and
wobbled with laughter.

88   A dream of breathing

I wandered home through Republic Park. The big high swooping
blue vague monument looked down at the little crowd as it
dispersed, like a giraffe inspecting dungbeetles.

That night I dreamed. A religious dispute. People that breathed
through their noses shouted mutely at people who breathed
through their mouths. They were all dressed in yellow dust.

89   Two nurses

I hurried up Ali Emiri 4. It was a warm, dull day and the streets
were puddled with last night's rain. The city walls were perfectly
black. I stood in a puddle as the day got warmer and warmer. By
conjoining the disparate phenomena of the world, by giving life to
the inanimate and wroughtness to the living, similes, like water-
drops gathering into rainfall in a cloud, are things of weight,
gravity and earth. I smiled at the shallow cloudiness of the sky. I
hurried towards the Weekday Health Centre.

The nurse was waiting with another, who had a clipboard with a
piece of grey paper clipped on it. She smiled at me with dazzling
white teeth. I bowed. The nurse slit open the cellophane on a new
box of syringes with her fingernail. Card please, said the other
nurse. I gave her the pink Rabies Record Card. The fridge burbled
and flickered. I'd miss it. She drew a line. No need to come back,
she said smilingly. The dogs are all quite healthy. She smiled again.
Her whiteness shone in the grey room. The watertaps dripped
silver drops. I smiled back.

I climbed into the couch. The swooping steel tubing squeaked and sighed. Oh, the last time. The nurse didn't say left left left. The other nurse watched her, and came nearer in a blur of white light and hovered over us. I shut my eyes. An injection is an injection is an injection. I opened them. The little window blurred white. The nurse waved the syringe. The other nurse smiled. The needle went in where it should, delivered its serum to the right places, and withdrew steelily. That's it, said the other nurse. She clipped the pink card on her clipboard. Get well soon, she said whitely.

I climbed out of the couch. I bowed at the nurse and shook her big hand. Her pearls popped with light. Her hair whirled. Thanks, I said. You're welcome, she said.

I was delivered out into the dullness of day. Perhaps they were all better too. The girl with her head wound round with bandages. The prisoner who smelt of mud. The little boy from Siirt with his foot tied up in a sheet. I raced home.

90   At the Great Mosque

I walked through the city smiling. I hurried to the Great Mosque. A wooden foldopen stall lit by a paraffin lamp opened its books in the porch. A man in a little white hat sat in front of the pair of high dark studded cracked wooden doors selling perfume in coloured bottles. The light from the paraffin lamp made them dance. I hurried inside. A blind man sitting on a folding chair on the uneven stones of the courtyard sang loudly. Lights from lanterns and electric chandeliers twinkled out from the rooms all round the yard. Water splashed at a fountain of taps. Under one chandelier I saw a man sitting on a carpet, all in white, bowed with his eyes closed in front of a microphone. I sat on the uneven stones. I didn't think of anything. What use was that? What could you do? There was no understanding it. If God lived in the hill. Or if he didn't.

I hurried out. Halfway out the door, near the red and green and yellow and blue bottles of the perfumeseller, I gave up the struc- ture of my soul to the random events it had always tried to make sense of. It just got so heavy.

91   And the reward was beauty

I ran up the steps on the city walls at Mardin Gate. I stood on top.
The whole world, seen from this high, was bushy and green. The
Dijle ran, silvergrey, through the bluegreen orchard trees and the
yellowgreen fields on the far bank. I walked up to the very edge. I
looked down. The university, the river, fields, orchards, groves of
straight slender aspens and the mountains. I smiled. Donkeys
grazed on the banks of earth that sloped gently up to the feet of the
city walls. In one completely black field crouched a woman
pricking out seedlings in the company of a white dog. I cried.

Suddenly, a horse and cart clattered out of the city, through the
city walls by the gate under my feet and shot out the other side
onto the Mardin road. A man completely white with flour
thrashed the horse pell-mell away down the road. He stood
unshakably upright on the tray of the cart, yanking the reins here
and there and bellowing. The horse threw up puffs of white dust. I
gasped. They thundered away into the evening.

I have never seen anything as good as that again.

Usually, I thought, a bit of me would try to go with them. But a
bit of them is still with me. That's good.

92   A man asleep

I sighed. Then I saw a man lying right on the edge of the wall–
tower a few feet away from me. He was fast asleep. A long stick lay
beside him. His boots turned up broken at the toes. Someone lit a
tilley lamp in the teahouse under the city walls. The man was
snoring lightly. Then a long line of white horses carrying bricks
clopped out through Mardin Gate and down the hill away from
Diyarbakir. I heard the little bells on their bridles. The road to.

93   A bunch of flowers and some other presents

The shoeshine boy did my shoes a kind of plastic grey. I paid him anyway. Fikri Dikmen took me to the Golden Flowershop by Republic Park. The big high swooping blue vague monument didn't do anything but look blue. And swooping. And. I bought fourteen red roses. The manager wrapped them in purple cellophane and hung them round with curly ribbons of pink silk. She smiled. I bowed. We hurried to the Weekday Health Centre. Roses and ribbons in the morning. Then I didn't feel silly. What use was that? Have a cigarette, said Fikri Dikmen. We hurried past the wiry tree. It stuck up twistedly. Two squiggles of smoke got pulled along behind us and drifted round the trunk. The big yellow crane creaked noddingly on the first floor. We hurried down the crumbly concrete steps.

I gave the flowers to the nurse. The other nurse smiled dazzlingly. They curtseyed. I bowed. Thank you very much, I said. You're welcome, said the nurse. The fridge burbled.

I climbed into the couch. I don't know. In slow motion, as if she were putting everything into a last performance, the nurse injected my stomach for the last time. While the other nurse drew another line across my pink Rabies Record Card further down. Had I already. 2ccs. She yanked out the needle with a kind of coy ferocity. Like a. I couldn't care less what happened in between.

We hurried back to Ali Emiri 4. The sun nuzzled against a misty whiteness in the air. We rounded the top of the street. A man with no legs sat on the pavement. A little wooden sledge tied under him by his stumps. His hands were all balled up in leather mittens wound round and round with bits of rag and sacking. He held his face up to the nuzzling sun and panted. In the morning, with the whole day ahead of him, I pitied him. We stopped. His olive eyes opened. Fikri Dikmen gave him two cigarettes. I gave him a handful of notes. He pushed the notes into his torn dusty darkblue coat. Fikri Dikmen lit his cigarette. The sun breathed on the misty whiteness and it cleared a bit. He swung his body into Ali Emiri 4 and ran on his fists through the dust. A horse and cart clattered round him. He bowled away down the road towards the city walls, punching the gravel. A squiggle of smoke pursued him. The city walls shone like tar in the new sun.

94   The last day of April

I dreamed in the night that Jem Murat told me fizzy lemonade gave him a sore throat. I slept late.

A bright blue hot day. The twisted gates shone. Ali Emiri 4 ran past like a. Birds trilled pleasantly through the trelliswork. The greening rosegarden distilled its rosy smell in the hot earth. My window sparkled. I hurried out. The sun hugged me warmly.

Nejati Bey was drinking tea in the Institute tearoom. He clacked his amber beads mournfully. The sun lit up the amber meniscus in his glass. It sparkled with sugar. I could hear Sevtap on the telephone saying yes yes over and over and over. The Director, I thought. Dr Ismail stumped in. He had just paid his fees. He smiled and frowned in a black and white checked jacket. I'll come at, he said frowningly, seven. I agreed whatever. He smiled. Good, he said. His jacket came and went. Now it's all over, he said frowningly. I bowed, surprised. Why? He'd said. Why him? Why not. He smiled. The sun explored his jacket in fits and starts. He left. Nejati Bey clacked his amber beads and looked at me sadly. He's a fascist, he said swirling his golden tea.

95   An evening out with Dr Ismail the army doctor

Dr Ismail came at seven. We wandered expansively in the warm evening air to the Army Medical Department Teahouse. The night air backstroked round the trees, which undulated their leaves and swayed their branches gently. Fairylights, all plain, twinkled in the trees. Like. Tremblingly. We drank our tea while Dr Ismail gently and smilingly stroked a map of Turkey pinned to our table with his pipestem everywhere he had ever been on holiday. I purred. Come on, he said frowning. His jacket stroboscoped under the fairylights. We rose into the Pilmen Resaurant in a lift. We drank tea and looked out over the modest lights of Diyarbakir. Dr Ismail smiled and puffed. His jacket jazzed around in the redplush furniture. Then we wandered expansively down Ali Emiri Not 4 to the Officers' Club. Its big marble box of floors was guarded by soldiers with machineguns and bayonets. We wandered in, pursued by Dr

Ismail's pipesmoke. We sat on shiny barstools and were given sodawater by a barman in a white jacket and shiny hair. Dr Ismail read me stories from the paper. A man had jumped off the city walls near Mardin Gate but had only broken his leg. There was a photo of him being led away handcuffed by the police. Arrested for his unwelcome declaration of private despair. The goal kings of the football league were photographed wearing crowns and erminetrimmed robes. Dr Ismail took out his pipe and buzzed in the sodawater. Listen to this, he said frowningly.

96   Mehmet the two-headed baby

Mehmet the two-headed baby had been born in a small village a few miles from Diyarbakir. His mother had disowned him straight away. She said he was a monster visited on her by evil spirits. The people in the village thought he was the devil. But his father had carried him in his arms to the State Hospital where Dr Shimshek was waiting. Dr Ismail paused and smiled. A mutual acquaintance, he said. Then he put his pipe back in and went on reading. A nurse said to the newspaper, everyone loves little Mehmet. In the days that followed a successful operation, removing one of the heads, was performed on little Mehmet, who was then adopted. Aren't people kind? said Dr Ismail smiling. His jacket couldn't make up its mind. Yes, I said, very. A lump in my throat. Now, said Dr Ismail frowningly, for a real drink. Cognac, he said smiling very much at the barman in the white jacket and shiny hair. Sorry sir, we haven't got any. Dr Ismail frowned. Gin will do, he said.

Then he had another one.

97   An old man

Dr Ismail puffed and checkered. A big TV screen showed a coloured picture of Trees near Malabadi Bridge for Ramadan. I stared. The screen got bigger. The trees were still and beautiful. The new green shoots shot out stilly. The screen started to curl around the room. The trees grew and grew without movement. Their roots burrowed in dark pebbly soil. It didn't look so nour-

119

ishing. I stood on a dark sandy pebbly bank. My shoes wobbled with little clatters. But the pebbles didn't move. The trees, completely still, looked solicitous and then just treelike. Not making up their minds. Like Dr Ismail's jacket. I walked amongst the slender trunks. They were flat as cardboard. The leaves bristled and fluttered stilly, coloured only on one side. What drove them to be trees? Why were they nothing but what they were made? I stepped carefully between two more. They looked beautiful and flat. I decided to dig in the ground. To see. I knelt on the pebbles and stuck my hand in the dirt. It felt like a flurry of paper. Or ashes. It shifted lifelessly. I burrowed in.

Suddenly I was in a white room. An towerblock room. An old man lay on a white divan against one wall. I shook his hand, which was long and white. A rush mat lay on the floor. Another old man sat against the far wall, crosslegged and grunting now and then. He was less white. Now and then he looked at his silver watch, which he pulled out of his waistcoat. Pinned on the wall was a Shell Company calendar with a picture of the silvery Bosphorus Bridge, so enormously beautiful that it looked like the path of an angel, from which flew red and white banners. There was a small window filled with blue sky. Across it now and then swivelled the heads of cranes like. Back and forth without a sound. Back and forth. I watched from the middle of the room. The old man unrolled a prayermat for the old man. It spoke in a faded voice of yellow, purple and red. Then he sat the old man up on the edge of his bed, put his feet on the mat and the bedcover round his shoulders. With his face held up at the bright square of sky and cranes, the old man prayed. His lips whispered. The old man looked at his silver watch.

98   Boing, halva and Military

Right, said Dr Ismail smilingly, let's go. But we didn't hurry. The TV screen shrank with a pleasant rubbery boing. I smiled. We puffed up further in the lift to the Restaurant. I had spicy raw meatballs. Dr Ismail smiled. I drank beer after beer. We looked out over the statue of Atatürk, which looked especially friendly in the twinkling lights, and the Council Bus Depot. Dr Ismail ate his stuffed vineleaves. A bus pulled away, yellowy inside. Let's go to Ergani! he said, and guffawed, haha. I smiled and drank beer. Who cares?

Then we had halva.

To finish the evening we strolled to the Children's Teagarden opposite the Post Office, smoking expansively. We drank five glasses of tea each under the trees on little children's chairs. Hundreds of neon tubes were strapped to the branches so that the canopy of trees above us looked like. The waiter was called Military. Dr Ismail snorted frowningly. Because, said Dr Ismail beaming, he was born when his father was on National Service. Oh dear! Can you imagine! His jacket laughed flickeringly. We decided to go on to the Green Garden Teahouse where we sat in the green garden under a rainbow of fairylights. Dr Ismail boomed with laughter. Military! he said, haha! I smiled.

For all sorts of reasons.

99   On and on and on and on

I walked home openmouthed with the world. How it just got on. Even I, with tiny regenerative wheels within wheels, was a part of its process. Eventually, I'd die. But not this time. Until then, miraculously repaired, I was still well.

100   Like

I wandered homewards. Some sheep looked down at me from someone's balcony. A big tree whispered. The moon swung out and up and over like.